HIP POCKET

CROSS WORDS

By Patrick Blindauer

PUZZLE
WRIGHT
PRESS

New York

**PUZZLE
WRIGHT
PRESS**

New York

An Imprint of Sterling Publishing
387 Park Avenue South
New York, NY 10016

2 4 6 8 10 9 7 5 3 1

Published by Sterling Publishing Co., Inc.
387 Park Avenue South, New York, NY 10016
© 2011 by Patrick Blindauer
Distributed in Canada by Sterling Publishing
c/o Canadian Manda Group, 165 Dufferin Street
Toronto, Ontario, Canada M6K 3H6
Distributed in the United Kingdom by GMC Distribution Services
Castle Place, 166 High Street, Lewes, East Sussex, England BN7 1XU
Distributed in Australia by Capricorn Link (Australia) Pty. Ltd.
P.O. Box 704, Windsor, NSW 2756, Australia

Printed in China

Sterling ISBN 978-1-4027-7749-3

For information about custom editions, special sales, premium and
corporate purchases, please contact Sterling Special Sales
Department at 800-805-5489 or specialsales@sterlingpublishing.com.

ADVICE TO TRAVELERS

ACROSS

1 1998 Paul Simon musical, with *The*
8 Refrain part
11 All excited
12 ___ sleep
13 Start of some travel advice from Hemingway
14 Music pub. giant
15 God, in Italy
16 Dollar alternative
17 Advice, part 2
22 Superman's adopted home
23 Advice, part 3
29 Fawning females?
30 Not mil.
31 Bedlam
32 Advice, part 4
36 Superlative ending
37 Bing Crosby or Al Bowlly, e.g.
38 Seminary subj.
39 Singing family of the 1970s

DOWN

1 "No problem"
2 Had a home-cooked meal
3 Basketball move
4 Acetyl ender
5 Bus. VIP
6 H.S. subject
7 Prefix with classical
8 Rome's ___ Fountain
9 Send, as payment
10 Mennonite group
16 *Horton Hears ___!*
18 Vintage vehicles
19 Writer Fleming
20 Nuptial starter
21 Mudhole
23 Puff snake
24 Hullabaloo
25 1983 Streisand role
26 Storrs school, for short
27 Did a jackknife
28 Once-___ (quick appraisals)
32 Cpl. or sgt.
33 *Chicago Hope* sets, for short
34 Hanks or Brokaw
35 Elton's john

BACK ORDER

ACROSS

1 Japanese sliding screen
6 Fools
11 Eva Duarte, after marriage
12 1950s trial
13 Kabul's country
15 Some greetings
16 *Damien* subtitle
19 Scale notes
22 People from the Twin Cities, e.g.
25 Baglike structure
26 Comparatively cockamamie
27 Play with the line "Brevity is the soul of wit"
30 Know-it-all
35 1998 De Niro film
36 Folding words
37 Specks
38 ___ Gritty Dirt Band

DOWN

1 Venue of indulgence
2 Bunny boss, briefly
3 Assn.
4 Bach or Strauss, e.g.
5 Bad way to be caught
6 ___ Tzu (toy dog)
7 "___ small world ..."
8 Citi Field goer
9 Free TV ad: Abbr.
10 R.R. stop
14 How some eat soup
16 Mantra syllables
17 Soccer star Hamm
18 Bewitch
20 It makes a man mean
21 Estonia, once: Abbr.
23 First point of contact in an alley, hopefully
24 Japanese mat
28 Operatic song
29 Cumberland ___ (Tenn. range)
30 Hindu title
31 Barn sound
32 "___ While I'm Around" (*Sweeney Todd* song)
33 When doubled, an expression of disapproval
34 Mudhole

CHEERS!

ACROSS

1 Vandalized, in a way
6 Beck's holder
11 Ready for a change
12 Fendi competitor
13 La Scala et al.
15 Mythical monster that's an anagram of a mythical bird
16 Talk, talk, talk
17 Dig into
18 Nutjob
20 Slight
22 Tony-winning musical of 1999
24 Playwright Bertolt
27 *Saving Private* ___
31 Creepy Chaney
32 Freshly painted
34 "___ Fool to Care" (1954 hit)
35 Warning sign
38 Dish for Oliver Twist
39 Sir Georg with a baton
40 Expertise
41 Mass follower?

DOWN

1 Kindle fodder
2 Hit the big leagues
3 ___-Roman wrestling
4 Suffix with puppet
5 6/6/1944
6 Wires on a bicycle wheel
7 Robert Morse theater role
8 Moves slowly and carefully
9 Standard of perfection
10 Very unpleasant
14 Pet store purchase
19 Popeye's alternative
21 ___ Lingus
23 "Them's the breaks!"
24 Construction co. projects
25 *The Fountainhead* hero Howard
26 World-weariness
28 Triangular traffic sign
29 Violin maker Nicolò
30 Gymnast Comaneci
33 Land under Down Under: Abbr.
36 Salon selection
37 Weed whacker

ELEMENTARY

ACROSS
1 One of the Dow Jones Industrials
4 Do nothing, with "out"
7 Pilot's update, for short
10 Mexican gold
11 Drink on draft
12 Flanders of *The Simpsons*
13 Saturated
16 Grace
17 Stetsons, e.g.
18 Perfect, as an alibi
21 Reg. version
24 Spot
25 Want ad inits.
26 April celebration
29 Puppets, e.g.
30 Part of a certain Macy's costume
34 Stephen King book made into a 1984 movie
37 "___ Beso" (Paul Anka song)
38 Running game
39 *Bad Behavior* star Stephen
40 Potential lifesaver, in brief
41 Decade divs.
42 Farthest from fore

DOWN
1 Hawkeye State
2 Thin fastener
3 Mr. ___ (Peter Lorre role)
4 Glossy coat
5 Conduit fitting
6 Prefix with political or logical
7 Captivate
8 Grow grinders
9 Enlarges
14 Oft-nicknamed period
15 Four, on the phone
19 McCarthy target
20 They get into hot water
21 Fixed price
22 Eastern philosophy
23 Timber problem
27 22-Down founder Lao-___
28 "Quit ___ joshin'!"
31 Razor name
32 Lagoon perimeter
33 Relative of "Fudge!"
35 Sow's pen
36 Road-paving stuff

JACKSON 5

ACROSS

1 Michael Jackson song of 1983
4 Calculating sort?
7 Michael Jackson song of 1972
10 Short head?
11 Dreamy state?
12 ___-Ida (frozen food brand)
13 Big jerk
14 Do a face plant
16 Nonnuclear family member
18 Plant twice
19 Miss, abroad: Abbr.
20 *Les Misérables* officer
21 Viper, for one
23 Office building area
26 Cassio's adversary
30 Supreme leader Ross
31 Williams of *Happy Days*
32 Dryly said
34 Had a little lamb
35 Resentment
36 Company perk
37 Arrest
38 Michael Jackson song of 1987
39 WSW's opposite
40 Jackson 5 song of 1970

DOWN

1 They may be laid out
2 First name in Mideast politics
3 Remote target?
4 Manitoba tribe
5 Word after split or snap
6 Acela Express runner
7 Oregon Trail city
8 Miscue
9 Cereal box stat.
15 Prepare, as shrimp
17 Dealer's workplace
20 Michael Jackson song of 1992
22 Subtle distinction
23 Improvise
24 Crownlike headgear
25 Did derbies
27 Yoga posture
28 Did pretty well in class
29 Last non-A.D. year
31 Forest measure
33 Holm of *Chariots of Fire*

ODD COUPLE

ACROSS

1 Judean king
6 Liszt piece
11 Stomach soother
12 Iced tea flavoring
13 *The Kraft Music Hall* regular
15 Backbreaking
16 Cloverleaf part
19 1558–1603 monarch: Abbr.
23 Korean car company
24 Watson's maker
26 "To Evening," e.g.
27 Learned
29 Iris cover
31 Actor Alain
33 Classic cartoon character
39 Valuable violin
40 Ernie Banks, familiarly
41 Is expected (to)
42 Egg parts

DOWN

1 *Oz* airer
2 Fence-sitters' sounds
3 Fabled *Arabian Nights* creature
4 Mutual of ___
5 Musical scale start
6 Atlas abbr.
7 *Fiddler on the Roof* role
8 Thurman of *Henry & June*
9 Button up, maybe
10 One treating a sinus infection, perhaps: Abbr.
14 Auto safety feature
16 Endorses
17 Peeples of *North Shore*
18 Unprestigious paper
20 Response to an online joke
21 Uganda's Amin
22 Overseas finale
25 "Well!"
28 Wife in *All in the Family*
30 Start of *el año*
32 It's a turnoff
33 ___ Schwarz
34 Six-foot Australian
35 Trail
36 250, Roman-style
37 Northern diving bird
38 Cable's "SuperStation"

S CARGO

ACROSS

1 Lead-in to hose or waist
6 Common bacterium
11 Russell of *Gladiator*
12 Feelings
13 Pile-up on a running track?
15 It's taken before swinging
16 It may be run up by drinking
19 Bad spots?
22 Cowley composition
23 2002 Olympics host: Abbr.
25 Schedule abbr.
26 Leaving a small opening
28 Irks
30 *Julius Caesar* setting
32 Made a movie about a yellow condiment?
37 Comedy legend Kovacs
38 Ready to read the riot act
39 1920s auto
40 Criminal subduer

DOWN

1 Dell products
2 Pioneering Dadaist
3 Easter preceder?
4 O. Henry plot specialty
5 Gossips
6 Fifty-fifty
7 Approximately
8 Expresses dissent
9 Idyllic place
10 Doctrine
14 Dramatic scene
16 Drag queen's wrap
17 Long or short, e.g.: Abbr.
18 Bases
20 Magic and Wizards org.
21 Satisfy the munchies
24 Watch a friend's feline
27 Adjust, as laces
29 Aquarium favorite
31 Chihuahua neighbor: Abbr.
32 Witness
33 Divs. of days
34 "___ in apple"
35 Mail no.
36 ___ Bingle (Crosby moniker)

THREE OF A KIND

ACROSS
1 Roadside jumpers: Abbr.
4 Forum 300
7 Wide shoe width
10 Fig. with two hyphens
11 Crowd for Caesar?
12 Lap dog
13 Riders on a carousel, maybe
15 Sign of a smash
16 Consider hilarious
18 Comics character who said "We have met the enemy and he is us"
21 Steamy, say
24 Second section
26 Gather, as cloth
27 For the time being
29 ___'acte (intermission)
30 Help with a loan
32 Weed killer
34 Anklebones
38 Financial fig.
39 Hugs, symbolically
40 Fade out
41 Sound from a wok
42 Net part, for short
43 Nodding noise

DOWN
1 Hand writing?: Abbr.
2 Sun Devils' sch.
3 Lee who directed *The Ice Storm*
4 "See ya!"
5 It may be in a poker player's hand
6 Some old Olds models
7 *Casablanca* screenwriter Julius
8 Where It.'s at
9 Maniac's problem?
14 Small cavern
17 2004 Olympics site
18 Very, very softly, in music
19 Galley tool
20 Food merchants
22 Richard Gere title role of 2000
23 Elementary letters?
25 Confer (upon)
28 Cat call: Var.
31 Cultivate
32 Calls one's own
33 Covert ___ (military job)
35 Chisellike tool
36 Actress Hurley, for short
37 "___ who?"

WASH ME

ACROSS

1 Member of the mint family
6 Come to ___
11 Old Oldsmobile model
12 Film not made by a major studio
13 With 14-Across, victorious streak
14 See 13-Across
15 Poetic contraction
16 Eight pts.
18 Sgt., e.g.
19 Where AT&T is T
21 Certain china collection
23 Rodeo tie
25 Shoot for, with "to"
28 *The Greatest American Hero* star William
32 Hagen who wrote *Respect for Acting*
33 Boastful talk
35 Needlefish
36 With 38-Across, an Eastwood role
38 See 36-Across
40 Santa Clara–based Fortune 500 company
41 Plans a getaway for, maybe
42 *Bells Are Ringing* composer Jule
43 Hospitality target

DOWN

1 Strip in the morning
2 Tennis court part
3 Prophets
4 *Deathtrap* writer Levin
5 ___ division
6 Bridal paths
7 Hurricane dir.
8 Elysian spots
9 Agnes, to Cecil B.
10 Train station
17 Out of port
20 Character actor Wallach
22 Apollo assent
24 Sock type
25 European autos
26 Tour of duty
27 Have a hootenanny
29 Conform (with)
30 Hardly prim sorts
31 Secret meeting
34 1970s hairdo
37 "Taps" time
39 *Aladdin* monkey

ATTENTION TO E-TAILS

ACROSS

1 "But of course!"
6 Triad, for example
11 Garden pest
12 One-third of a phrase meaning "etc."
13 Attractive appeals?
15 Honor
16 Speakeasy owner's fear
18 Divided English county
22 It has a husk
23 Call for help
24 Middle digit in all five ZIP codes of Beverly Hills
25 Marketplace
27 High spot
28 Truman portrayer of 1995
30 King of clawed crustaceans?
35 Gluck hero
36 Reagan attorney general
37 "Octopus's Garden" songwriter
38 Barber's accessory

DOWN

1 Get a little shuteye
2 Shower time: Abbr.
3 Luxury hotel, familiarly
4 Given a ticket
5 Sharp image producer, briefly
6 Island nation south of Turkey
7 Nathan and Alan
8 Lines from Shelley
9 Nutritional inits.
10 Putin's assents
14 "Decide already!"
16 Burgle
17 Source of gas, perh.
19 Noted gatekeeper
20 She-sheep
21 Noughts-and-crosses line
23 Anchor man?
26 Up actor Ed
27 Balance sheet plus
29 Some old laptops
30 Calendar pages: Abbr.
31 Pop or Dada
32 "___ tree falls ..."
33 That, to Tomás
34 Dem.'s foe

BREW HA-HA

ACROSS

1 Former Guns N' Roses guitarist whose real name is Saul Hudson
6 Opposite of *unter*
10 Point of orbital extreme
11 Iditarod terminus
12 Quip, part 1
13 Quip, part 2
14 Test versions
15 Part of a play
16 "Gee," in Glasgow
17 Modern conference beginning
19 Quip, part 3
24 Shoot
25 Stroke, say
26 With swiftness
29 Food in a nursery rhyme
31 Quip, part 4
32 Quip, part 5
33 Dear one, in Italy
34 They ride on lifts
35 Put aboard
36 Requirements

DOWN

1 Public address
2 Detest with a burning passion
3 Orinoco flow
4 Works with words, in a way
5 "___, good lookin'!"
6 Kid-helping org.
7 Speaker brand
8 Relative key of G maj.
9 Russo who played Natasha in the 2000 film *The Adventures of Rocky and Bullwinkle*
10 One with monk business
15 Slug
18 Wide shoe spec
20 There may be money in it
21 Went to market?
22 Jerks, in *Strange Brew*
23 Some jugs
26 Kid stuff
27 ___ moss
28 Prefix with dynamic
30 Nobelist Wiesel
32 QVC alternative

DOUBLE TROUBLE

ACROSS

1 Arabic for "peace"
7 Part of AMPAS: Abbr.
11 Wagner heroine
12 Yvette's evening
13 1978 Foreigner album
14 Delayed reaction
15 Prime the pot
16 Title character in an old ABC sitcom
18 Snout
20 2001 title role for Sean Penn
21 Betray
24 Mole
26 WWII general ___ Arnold
27 Prefix with suction
29 Film director's cry
31 Sonogram area
35 Fat under the face
36 Nested pot used for melting chocolate
38 "Shucks"
39 Surfing the Net
40 She met Rick in Paris
41 Deleted

DOWN

1 The Destroyer, in Hinduism
2 Alphabet book words
3 Neil Simon's ___ in Yonkers
4 They upset xenophobes
5 Much ___ About Nothing
6 Fixes
7 Fictional wirehair
8 Not fine-grained
9 Super Bowl XXVII MVP
10 Unreal
17 Multitude
19 Norway's capital
21 Happy Days part
22 TV friend of Phoebe and Monica
23 Science of vision
25 Lose it
28 Tray containing work to do
30 Start of a Jimmy Durante song
32 Mixture
33 Waiter's offering
34 Baseball's Saberhagen
37 Leading figure?

LETTER HEAD

ACROSS

1 Deer sirs
6 Privy fixture
11 First name in TV talk
12 Of concern to beekeepers
13 Atlantic City, e.g.
15 Old dogs
16 Most secure
19 "So, it's *you*!"
21 With 22-Across, something citric to steep and sip
22 See 21-Across
24 "So's ___ old man!"
25 *Jesus Christ Superstar* role
26 Accompanies to the airport, say
29 *Rocky III* theme
33 Turn on the dramatics
34 Start of an expiration notice
35 Biology class about birds and bees?
36 Suffix with xeno-

DOWN

1 ___ Sec.
2 "Decorates" on Halloween, briefly
3 *Exodus* hero ___ Ben Canaan
4 Thingie
5 "I can't believe it!"
6 Singer/activist Joan
7 ___ dixit
8 Miniature display
9 You can't hear if you're out of it
10 It may give you a charge
14 Like Gen. Powell
16 No place for a neatnik
17 "Sweet!"
18 1982 Clint Eastwood movie
20 *Arnie* actress Sue ___ Langdon
22 Elate
23 Small and mischievous
25 *The Murders in the Rue Morgue* writer
27 Rock back?
28 Mower site, maybe
29 -y, pluralized
30 Prefix with graphic or metric
31 Flow back
32 It may be seeded

OPPOSITES ATTRACT

ACROSS

1 Pre-calculator calculators
6 Thingie
11 *Aida* selections
12 Lion in Lewis's *The Chronicles of Narnia*
13 *¡Three Amigos!* actor
15 "Good morrow, cousin," for Romeo
16 Paycheck deduction
17 Actress Farrow
18 Highway entry
20 Chicken site
21 "Unhand me!"
23 Sentry's cry
26 Brightness measurer
30 Area of 1940s mil. activity
31 Ledger abbr.
32 Milne marsupial
33 *Cheers* actress
36 Mandel of *Deal or No Deal*
37 Speaking spots
38 Elizabeth I's ill-fated favorite
39 Suits

DOWN

1 Transmission franchise
2 Electric razor brand
3 Network, e.g.
4 Siamese ___
5 Introspective query
6 Mylanta alternative
7 Suffix like -esque
8 Replay technique
9 Tenor Lanza
10 Straight from the keg
14 Break for a nanny
19 Ctrl-___-Delete
20 Primitive sleeping spot
22 Metrosexual, e.g.
23 Pronoun with a slash
24 One of the Musketeers
25 Cinema chain
27 Lose ground?
28 Hedgehog of video game fame
29 *Animal House* costume pieces
31 *Family Ties* son
34 Bit of slander
35 Bagel shop offering

BATTLE OF THE SEXES

ACROSS

1 Garbage
6 Steal
11 Simmons competitor
12 ___ Remus
13 Best Picture of 1981, with *The*
15 Sn, to a chemist
16 Part of speech: Abbr.
17 Harris and Sullivan
18 Con
20 It goes back and forth in the woods
22 "Rock On" rocker David
24 1974 film shot from a dog's-eye view
28 Twisted
30 Bruce Springsteen, with "the"
31 Big Blue
34 Moody's best
36 DiMaggio stat
37 Oscar-nominated film of 1990
40 Navel variety
41 ___ change
42 Mount
43 Hawaiian entertainer

DOWN

1 African menace
2 Archaeological booty
3 Bowl sites
4 Engine additive letters
5 A few laughs
6 Land south of Kashmir
7 It borders James Bay: Abbr.
8 Top of the heap
9 Not nude
10 Egg layers
14 Marketing tools
19 Cry from a litter
21 Spider's work
23 Adult
25 Bates of *Psycho*
26 Composer of the *St. Matthew Passion*
27 Digs
29 "Whoopee!"
31 Wall St. announcements
32 Old Spice alternative
33 Distribute, with "out"
35 Knocked out
38 Fan letdown
39 Kitchen brand

TITLE PAGE

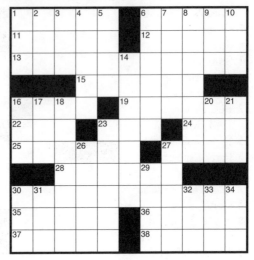

ACROSS

1 Chump
6 Take place
11 Gone, in a way
12 Almost ready for the tooth fairy
13 Anne Bancroft role of 1967
15 Relative of a tie
16 Take an ax to
19 Magnavox alternative
22 One may be bookmarked
23 Neighbor of Swe.
24 Actress Long or Peeples
25 Fashion designer Pucci
27 Bus. heads
28 1960s dance
30 Tap-dancer of song
35 ___ Vista Lake, California
36 *Franny and ___*
37 Kaufman and Warhol
38 Glade targets

DOWN

1 Religious school: Abbr.
2 Aries or Taurus, e.g.
3 Shaker ___, Ohio: Abbr.
4 Pharmaceutical giant
5 ___ about (roughly)
6 1968 Oscar-winning musical
7 *___ the Barbarian*
8 Going for
9 Mil. entertainers
10 Stimpy's animated pal
14 Rocket launcher
16 Cry's companion
17 Common place for a tattoo
18 Ascended
20 Director Burton or Robbins
21 Derby, for one
23 Martial arts masters
26 Nuts
27 "Holy cow!"
29 Carmaker Ferrari
30 Advanced deg.
31 Smuggle
32 Head of England?
33 Always, odically
34 Pt. of PBS

CITY LIGHTS

ACROSS

1 Unveiled
6 Some religious observances
11 McDonald of *Ragtime* on Broadway
12 Like venture capital investments
13 Elite military members
15 Coastal catch
16 Foreign refusal
19 Dark time, maybe
24 "Let your fingers do the walking" book
26 People in *People*
27 Polite fellow
28 Baloney
30 Sophie Tucker claimed to be the last one, in a song
37 Name in a 2002 scandal
38 *Odyssey* follows it
39 Extraterrestrial, e.g.
40 Approaching the hour

DOWN

1 Wilt
2 Ben-___
3 Words from Wordsworth
4 Try for a pin
5 Second starter?
6 Make available
7 Cause of inflation?
8 Fresno-to-L.A. dir.
9 B'way purchase
10 Modus operandi: Abbr.
14 Fails majorly
16 Columbia Univ. locale
17 "___-haw!" (cry of delight)
18 Pipe bend
20 Bargain hunter's destination
21 Live longer?
22 Joint Chiefs member: Abbr.
23 Body shop fig.
25 Shaped like a fish stick
29 Give off
30 Johnny ___
31 Suffix with acetyl
32 Soft & ___ (Gillette product)
33 Dear
34 Hour div.
35 Yoga surface
36 Busy activity

FORD DEALERSHIP

ACROSS

1 In ___ (befuddled)
6 ___ Ford
11 Charge with more duties
12 Captivate the crowd, perhaps
13 When Macbeth slays Duncan
14 Gain succulence
15 Ford ___ (Andrew Dice Clay role)
17 Goes along
18 Orch. section
21 Bath water tester
22 Manhattan's east/west arteries: Abbr.
24 Done, to Donne
26 Foreign policy gp.
28 Low Countries locale
30 ___ Ford
32 Like about 13% of Americans
35 Chicken feed
36 Hebrew title of respect for God
37 Pigeons' place
38 ___ Ford
39 MIT part: Abbr.

DOWN

1 One of *Time*'s 1993 Man of the Year winners
2 Ten-sided shape
3 Arrays
4 Old name for Kinshasa's country
5 Banishes
6 Little Boy Blue's instrument
7 Great Lakes Indians
8 Flannel feature
9 I-85, e.g.
10 Hankering
16 Part of a certain belt
19 Prematurely
20 Homework assignments
23 Big ___
25 Milk curdler
27 20th anniversary symbol
29 Christina of *The Opposite of Sex*
31 Uptight
32 Time difference
33 Fruity drink suffix
34 Craggy hill

PET NAMES

ACROSS

1 Risotto alternative
6 "You look like you've seen a ___!"
11 *All My Children* regular
12 Jeweler's glass
13 Diagonal (to)
15 Had something, so to speak
16 Be off base
17 Nanny ___
18 Foam toy brand
20 Edmonton hockey team
22 Satisfy a debt
24 Peer (at)
27 NYC's ___ River
31 Jerome Kern's "___ Song"
32 Facility with a monkey house
34 "Nope"
35 Slow way to swim
38 1980s TV group
39 ___ cards
40 Everglades grass
41 Carnivorous cackler

DOWN

1 Pie ingredient, perhaps
2 Not just peeved
3 Two-thirds of a magnum
4 Perform in plays
5 Alice of old musicals
6 *All in the Family* role
7 Opposite of vert.
8 Shot glass capacity, roughly
9 *Avatar* weapon
10 Contract specs
14 Shirt leaving the midriff exposed
19 You may thank God for it: Abbr.
21 Potassium hydroxide
23 Pepsin, for one
24 Boston pops?
25 Nasdaq listing
26 Pressed
28 ___ the Giant (*The Princess Bride* actor)
29 Permanent place
30 Certain sorority woman
33 Swear words
36 Funny bit
37 Justice Sandra ___ O'Connor

B&B

ACROSS

1 Pond fish
4 Rotten
7 Jacques or Jeanne
10 Announcement at JFK: Abbr.
11 Mount Suribachi site
13 Heart rate reducer
15 Riyadh resident
16 Tennille of the Captain and Tennille
17 Start of everything, theoretically
21 Codebreakers' org.
22 Microscopic creature
24 Not well-defined
27 Gaffer's assistant
31 Key with four sharps: Abbr.
33 Badlands feature
34 What the anxious wait with
38 Mold in the freezer?
39 *The Matrix* hero
40 General on Chinese menus
41 "___ Loves You"
42 Sold-out sign

DOWN

1 Meat on a stick
2 Cheri of *Inspector Gadget*
3 Convention handout
4 Baby's tie-on
5 Shoemaker's tool
6 Scooby-___
7 Camera brand
8 Portents
9 *West Side Story* song
12 Highway sign abbr.
14 "Chiquitita" band
18 State Dept. figure
19 Maiden name indicator
20 *Pygmalion* playwright's monogram
23 "Ma! He's Making Eyes ___"
24 Payment option
25 Some computers
26 Spanish saint
28 Word after jelly or coffee
29 Blender maker
30 "Hurray!"
32 Leave, slangily
35 Cutting-room staff?: Abbr.
36 Dickensian cry
37 Tavern order

CROSS WORDS

ACROSS

1 Showed wonderment
6 Political pundit Bill
11 Impolite look
12 "There Is Nothin' Like ___"
13 Eyebrow makeup
14 First *Survivor* winner Richard
15 *Number Four, Bobby ___!* (kids' book)
16 *The Mikado* costume piece
18 Canadian capital?
19 Informed about
21 Father of Elam and Aram
22 They're set in hospitals
24 Ty of Cooperstown
27 Part of an order
31 LaGuardia posting: Abbr.
32 Fla. setting
33 Takes too much
34 Animal variety
36 They have shoulders
38 Feudal lord
39 Actress MacDowell
40 Not broadside
41 Sits for snaps

DOWN

1 "Let's have ___ of hands"
2 Electronic game pioneer
3 They may be split
4 Go off track
5 Mississippi River explorer
6 When repeated, a dolphinfish
7 Letters on a toothpaste tube
8 See 25-Down
9 Party leader, maybe
10 Shorten again, perhaps
17 Archeological find
20 Shrink from shore
21 Retired speedster
23 Snare
24 Dish alternative, maybe
25 With 8-Down, longtime senator from Utah
26 Afghan, for one
28 Arteries
29 Actor Murphy
30 Lots of sass?
32 Fall venue
35 It may get a boost
37 One "virgin" of *Two Virgins*

IN OR OUT

ACROSS
1 "___ we dance?"
6 ___ *Majesty's Secret Service*
11 Jack of *The Great Dictator*
12 Jelly fruit
13 Title character in a 1998 Spielberg movie
15 Presidential inits.
16 Simulated
17 Grammy-winning Twain
19 Red letters?
20 Tell (from)
22 Unofficial news source
25 ___ *and Geeks*
29 Permit to enter
31 Latin possessive
32 Dillinger, once
34 Impossible to improve upon
35 Pix
36 "Try to ___ my way ..."
37 Fifty minutes past

DOWN
1 Campus class, informally
2 Like an unfiltered cigarette
3 Dog with a curled-back tail
4 Actress Tyler
5 "___ lizards!" ("Little Orphan Annie" line)
6 Molding shape
7 Take under one's wing
8 Garfield's predecessor
9 Cowgirl Dale
10 Downtime, so to speak
14 2000 Soderbergh film
18 Composer Rimsky-Korsakov
21 A Gallo brother
22 Blue shade
23 Get away from
24 *Tiny Alice* playwright
26 "You're ___ one, Mr. Grinch ..."
27 Well-groomed
28 Final word
30 Shrivel
33 About one o'clock: Abbr.

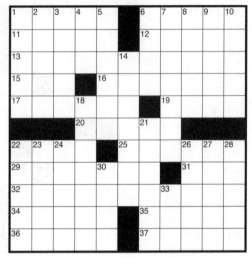

OXYMORONS

ACROSS

1 Maui neighbor
6 "A stitch in time saves nine," for example
11 Mushroom cloud maker
12 Moves, as cars
13 Like some memories
15 *Money* mgrs.
16 Wasn't cooped up
17 Pope who crowned Charlemagne emperor
19 They pass the bucks
20 ___ passages
22 Effuse
25 Most cool, in rap slang
29 Words of denial
31 *Blue Hawaii* costume piece
32 Cocktail component
34 Spring locale
35 Nin who wrote *Delta of Venus*
36 Tickle pink
37 Fresh

DOWN

1 Record company
2 Tolerate
3 "___ fast!"
4 Tsp. or tbsp.
5 It's south of the Pyrenees
6 Org.
7 Time when the grass gets damp
8 Warn
9 Aquafresh alternative
10 ___ Park, Colorado
14 Stuffing ingredients
18 Restrain
21 Hellos (or goodbyes) in the 50th state
22 Action hero since '64
23 Bar patron's request, with "the"
24 Kafka's *Metamorphosis* hero Gregor
26 Inventor Howe
27 Big rigs
28 Slightly soused
30 Teaspoonful, maybe
33 Genetic inits.

THE I'S HAVE IT

ACROSS

1 "___ be my pleasure!"
4 Elton John, e.g.
7 FX technology
10 Hosp. procedure
11 DH's stat
12 Street sign abbr.
13 Concealed
14 Real-time e-notes
15 Show set in Vegas
16 Schools for engrs.
18 Wrap-arounds
20 Heart of the matter
21 Maze goal
22 Last Supper query
24 Russian pancakes
27 Some contractions
31 Driving courses?
32 Long Island town near Bay Shore
33 Type
34 Country place
36 Sale tag abbr.
37 Added to 7-Down, 1402
38 TV news time
39 Dernier ___ (last word)
40 Spare part?
41 State Farm's bus.
42 Web search result

DOWN

1 Cat's comment of understanding
2 "Lemon Tree" singer Lopez
3 Shakespearean verb with "thou"
4 Hindu titles
5 Corporate inits. since 1924
6 Take the chance
7 See 37-Across
8 Basic ideas
9 Like a brogue
17 "Concentrate!"
19 Monogram parts: Abbr.
21 Hi-___
23 "Most certainly, señor!"
24 Soaring sight at the Super Bowl
25 Palmer of *The Gentle Sex*
26 Make permanent, as a cartoon
28 Peter ___ Tchaikovsky
29 Wispy clouds
30 Sail spar
32 1980s rock band from Australia
35 *Little Birds* author

CON-JUNCTIONS

ACROSS

1 1066 loser
6 Having eyes, poetically
11 Informed (of)
12 Reeves of *Speed*
13 Twangy genre
14 Grocery chain
15 Youngster
16 Put to the test
18 ___ diligence
19 Ophthalmological case
21 "___ Fables"
23 Cable channel
25 Neither gaseous nor solid
28 "See you"
32 Gasteyer of *SNL*
33 Sp. woman
35 Insurance co.
36 Money lender, for short
38 Love letter letters
40 Put on, as a character
41 Nash of note
42 Peruses
43 Fit for page one

DOWN

1 Spud bags
2 Anticipate
3 Standard graph axes
4 O'Hare's airport code
5 Eye of ___ (witches' brew ingredient)
6 Sanctioned
7 Stephen of *V for Vendetta*
8 Monopoly railroad
9 "This ___" (carton label)
10 Fools
17 Time off, briefly
20 Arles water
22 Prepared
24 Supermarket spots
25 Tattoo remover
26 Senseless
27 Informal interview
29 Soft drink name
30 Ocean phenomena
31 *Into the Woods* duet between Cinderella's Prince and Rapunzel's Prince
34 Impulse transmitter
37 It fizzles
39 "Act your ___!"

FOUR QUARTERS

ACROSS

1 Had something substantial
7 Off base, perhaps
11 "Well, then ..."
12 Joan of art
13 One of four quarters
14 Resurgently
15 Kyoto treaty subj.
16 Rasputin, for one
18 Oahu hootenanny
20 Part of a school's web site name
21 *Hamlet* and *Othello*
24 Diamond weight
26 Marker
27 ___ Fifth Avenue
29 Mother ___
31 Kind of foot
35 Breakfast item in old Rome?
36 One of four quarters
38 Work between jobs
39 Cry from Juliet
40 Some IDs
41 Turning points

DOWN

1 It has your name on it: Abbr.
2 Potentially insulting
3 Lighting specialist, informally?
4 ___ cheesesteak
5 Age
6 Upheld conviction?
7 *Amo, ___, amat* (Latin exercise)
8 One of four quarters
9 Major name in frozen foods
10 Revealing, as a dress
17 "Ew!"
19 One of the Allies of WWII
21 Dry reds
22 Elements of a biblical miracle
23 One of four quarters
25 *I, Robot* author
28 Ancient moralist
30 Diamond experts
32 Contents of some barrels
33 Make the acquaintance of
34 Warner ___
37 William Tell's canton

MUSICAL TRIO

ACROSS

1 Idiosyncrasy
4 Knight's title
7 Siesta time: Abbr.
10 First name in dictators
11 Sound-activated switch
13 Eight-time Best Actor nominee
15 Final decision
16 Some pipe joints
17 View in northern Italy
20 Flower on a French shield
21 *The Capeman* composer
24 Disney collectible
25 Net-surfer's stop
26 Bookie's concern
28 "Take a sip"
32 Her most famous work is subtitled *The Modern Prometheus*
35 Signal light
36 Leader in a suit?
37 1040 ID

38 Onscreen pop-ups
39 Beta rival, once

DOWN

1 Loses verticality
2 Noodle product?
3 ___ hall
4 Moves with a mouse, maybe
5 U.N. agcy. for working people
6 Dirty dog
7 Harlem theater
8 Collapsed
9 Head lock

12 "The Gold-Bug" writer
14 Genesis twin
18 Next-to-last Greek letter
19 Caretakers
21 Car controls
22 Buzz in space
23 Square ___
24 Honey bunch?
27 Prefix with thesis
29 Czech, e.g.
30 Georgia ___
31 Looks at
33 Schuss or wedel
34 ___ and haw

SAME SURNAME

ACROSS

1 With 22-Across, *All About Eve* star
6 With 22-Across, trumpeter of note
11 A.k.a.
12 When Plácido Domingo was born
13 Jazz genre
14 ___ *Cakes* (Food Network show)
15 "___ Maria"
16 Louvre affair?
18 Nutritional std.
19 Where rods and cones are
21 Parting words
22 Common surname
24 Elusive creature
27 Takes back the lead?
31 Earlier
32 Thesaurus abbr.
33 151, in Caesar's day
34 Cuba's leader?
36 The Fab Four, e.g.
38 Hateful disgrace
39 Chamber piece
40 With 22-Across, *Do the Right Thing* actor
41 With 22-Across, *Beetlejuice* star

DOWN

1 Elephant of kid lit
2 École attendee
3 Where the Brahmaputra flows
4 Principle of philosophy
5 *Madrileño*'s land
6 Gist
7 Like Bach's Sonata No. 3 for violin
8 Distrustful
9 Gradually remove
10 Chesterfields
17 Carried on
20 Ugandan despot Amin
21 Blue & Gold Banquet gp.
23 Berlin who wrote "Puttin' On the Ritz"
24 Boorish person
25 Affected outburst
26 Amos and Spelling
28 Bakery goodie
29 Comedienne DeGeneres
30 "Soul ___" (Bilal tune)
32 Highest point
35 Motoring offense, briefly
37 Mr. X

SURROUNDED BY BEES

ACROSS

1 Some mowers
6 *Goodbye, Mr. Chips* star Robert
11 Dangling part of the soft palate
12 Name on a bomber
13 Site of an ill-fated tower
14 *Cowboy* ___ (anime series)
15 Prior to
16 Play the part
18 Filmmaker Spike
19 Go-getter
21 Tudor nickname
22 Authoritative text
24 Bathroom supply
27 Tot
31 Prefix with -tard
32 *China Beach* setting, for short
33 "Hold On Tight" band
34 U.K. lawman
36 ___ Gump Shrimp Company
38 Special qualities
39 Have ___ for
40 Compete in the Winter Olympics, maybe
41 Parts

DOWN

1 Went with the flow, in a way
2 Female gland
3 *American Idol* winner Studdard
4 Sporting event shout
5 "Go hang a ___; I'm a lasagna hog!" (palindrome)
6 Card balance
7 A quarter of four
8 High-minded
9 Lily family plants
10 Cassettes
17 Striking snake
20 *Lost* network
21 "I ___ your pardon!"
23 Kind of vertebra
24 Oompah instruments
25 Actress Aimée
26 The Scales, astrologically
28 James Dean persona
29 *Seascape* playwright
30 Stool sitters?
32 Trading letters
35 Halloween decoration
37 Numero ___

TWO SURE THINGS

ACROSS

1 Some shells
6 Nigerian city
11 Ocean menaces
12 Heroine of Turgenev's *On the Eve*
13 Californian desert basin
15 1986 #1 hit for Starship
16 Pilot
17 Academic stretch
19 Civil War inits.
22 "___ gather"
23 Seat holders
24 Nectar sources
27 Heated arguments
28 1939 film home
32 How some things may be deducted
34 Mature
35 Some vacation destinations
36 Library requests
37 Grand ___ Auto (video game series)

DOWN

1 They're full of beans
2 The Deep South, e.g.
3 Feature on Harry Potter's forehead
4 Exit lines, in Exeter
5 Baseball bat material
6 "Don't touch!"
7 "Come back— ___ forgiven"
8 *Ristorante* desserts
9 1310, off base
10 Grid great Gale
14 Split
18 Ones providing arms
19 "Rock the ___"
20 Swimwear company founded in Australia
21 The ___ Dodger (*Oliver Twist* character)
25 "___ you so!"
26 Secreted stuff
29 Rod for a hot rod
30 Natural breakwater
31 Gofer: Abbr.
33 Songbird

CAR TALK

ACROSS

1 Shade darker than chestnut
6 Remedies
11 Big name in dental hygiene
12 Barbara's role on *Dallas*
13 *Show Boat* song
15 When Dijon's hot
16 Bitter beverage
17 "Stand" band
18 Try
20 Concert hall cry
22 Noted stage role of 1949
24 *Baywatch* event
27 *When Harry Met Sally*... screenwriter Ephron
31 The Red Baron, e.g.
32 Demolitionist's supply
34 Common test subject
35 Lionel purchases
38 Beach, *en español*
39 Wear away gradually
40 Tendon
41 It borders Sudan and Tanzania

DOWN

1 Cleaning brand
2 Emulate Webster
3 Bars of soap
4 Cheer at the end of a dance
5 Eban of Israel
6 Montana's capital
7 Roth who directed *Hostel*
8 Old Oldsmobile
9 ___ and onions
10 Summons from the boss
14 It's found in a table
19 Infant's need, for short
21 Media inits. since 1980
23 One who's wanted
24 Hospital egresses
25 Sanitation worry
26 Four-door
28 Constellation next to Taurus
29 Newman who won an Oscar for *Monsters, Inc.*
30 Where "ahoy!" is heard
33 Hard journey
36 See
37 "Who ___ we kidding?"

FROM EAR TO EAR

ACROSS
1 Certain shindig
6 Fauna's partner
11 Stevenson of 1950s politics
12 Cable channel
13 Result of normal use
15 Plato's language
16 News office
19 Grub
23 Doc bloc
24 MO town
26 Big ___
27 Stocking, in heist movies
29 Alfalfa, for one
31 Companionless
33 Close
39 Intensified, as sound
40 Transmission chain
41 Spring
42 Accord

DOWN
1 Like sushi
2 Keats work
3 Miss. neighbor
4 One who answers to a looie
5 Jeweled headpieces
6 Lose color
7 Kosher deli offering
8 Four quarters
9 Vitamin info: Abbr.
10 Bubbly beginning?
14 Atomic particle
16 "Kapow!"
17 John's *Pulp Fiction* dance partner
18 Dorm watchers, for short
20 *One Life to Live* airer
21 Chai, e.g.
22 It has a wkly. guest host
25 Martin who played Bela Lugosi in *Ed Wood*
28 Allen of *Raiders of the Lost Ark*
30 Park Avenue, e.g.
32 Great Gatsby player of 1949
33 Capture
34 Rock subgenre
35 Kwik-E-Mart clerk on *The Simpsons*
36 Record inits.
37 Undertaking
38 Writer ___ Blount Jr.

ORIENTATION

ACROSS

1 *The Hobbit* character
6 Special delivery
11 Out-and-out
12 Six months from *julio*
13 Cushion projection, maybe
15 More revolting
16 Popular pens
19 Join the navy, say
22 Eminem ___ Slim Shady
23 Little League coach, often
24 Round Table title
25 Wing-footed one
27 Like Sadie, in a song
28 Quimby of kid lit
30 *Hello, Dolly!* time period
35 They're found among the reeds
36 Car care company
37 Al ___ (not too soft)
38 Perdue rival

DOWN

1 School vehicle
2 Hairy TV cousin
3 Paper size: Abbr.
4 Boyfriends
5 Something copied: Abbr.
6 Trailing
7 Silicon Valley name
8 Musical ending, often
9 Prefix with lateral or lingual
10 Sweetums
14 Fats portrayer in *The Hustler*
16 "___, humbug!"
17 War-hero prez
18 "Proceed!"
20 Three safeties' score
21 "___ to Remember" (opening number of *The Fantasticks*)
23 End
26 *The Asparagus* painter
27 Skewered Thai dish
29 Peachy-keen
30 25-Across, e.g.
31 Honest prez
32 Chats online, for short
33 Logical intro?
34 23-Across's boy

SOUND STAGE

ACROSS

1 Sale locale
7 Slightly open
11 Midsized Oldsmobiles
12 Gimlet garnish
13 Smashing
14 Doing what needs to be done
15 Got up
16 Damp
17 Policy reversal
19 Roman 205
22 *For the Boys* gp.
23 Dir. from Toledo to Akron
24 Sound of an approaching horse
27 Corrective eye surgery
28 Explosive, informally
32 Tyrant Idi
33 Modern music genre
34 Member of an order
35 "In ___ and out the other"
36 Wolves, for wolfhounds
37 *Sweet Rosie* ___ (Betty Grable film)

DOWN

1 Gangsters' guns
2 Came down
3 ___ *Man* (1984 movie)
4 Sun Tzu's *The ___ War*
5 "Break a leg!"
6 Purported ability
7 Uninvolved
8 Campaign tune
9 Mexican pals
10 Key in again
16 Nestled front-to-back
18 Part of some chains: Abbr.
19 Gadget for gripping
20 Hubbub
21 Tetrahydrozoline brand
25 Little finger
26 March 17 marcher
29 ___-*Team* (2010 Liam Neeson film)
30 Intersection part
31 Word after "Ole"
33 Sob syllable

X-FACTOR

ACROSS

1 Vet's memory, perhaps
4 Six-pt. scores
7 Gift from a wahine
10 Prefix with sphere
11 See 27-Down
12 Abbr. on some business letters
13 Item made of raw material?
16 Pavarotti, e.g.
17 "Luka" singer Suzanne
18 Role for Denzel
21 Directly across from: Abbr.
24 It follows leap day: Abbr.
25 Encl. to an editor
26 Gag glasses
29 French pop music of the 1960s
30 Pop singer Mann
34 They came after the boomers
37 Producer for U2 and Coldplay
38 Upset
39 "Little" singer of the sixties
40 Queensland neighbor: Abbr.
41 One over a birdie
42 Pathetic beginning?

DOWN

1 Casting director's dismissal
2 Fair-sized garden
3 Gripe
4 St. Louis squad
5 Father figure
6 Personal ad abbr.
7 Carpentry tools
8 "Hmm" inducer
9 Tool for Edmund Hillary
14 Author Clancy
15 Ab ___ (anew)
19 Drink like a dog
20 Mastermind
21 Word with tank or mask
22 Congratulates oneself
23 Gas station sign
27 With 11-Across, a cry of delight
28 Top of a clock dial
31 Homer's hangout
32 It "slayeth the silly one": Job
33 Crammer's worry
35 Shoot the breeze
36 Tooth docs' org.

AFTER "AFTER"

ACROSS

1 Hard rock, maybe
4 Hard-rock connection
7 "Amazing!"
10 Paving stuff
11 TiVo forerunner
12 Brouhaha
13 After "after," reconsideration
15 Hitchcock title
16 "___ go bragh!"
17 Blew out candles, maybe
19 10K, e.g.
20 Cookout leftover?
21 After "after," washroom product
23 After "after," how net gains are calculated
27 Something to dial: Abbr.
29 Breathing sound
30 Land created by C.S. Lewis
33 Rolling ___ (rich)
34 Musical Yoko
35 After "after," later on
37 Accepts
38 A billion years
39 Go out, as a flame
40 Glasgow refusal
41 ___ Peres (St. Louis suburb)
42 Western tribesman

DOWN

1 Web-footed animals
2 Like some peppy pep rally participants
3 1804 symphony
4 Dow Jones fig.
5 Pronunciation indicator
6 Chuck Close, e.g.
7 Clean
8 Jon Arbuckle's dog
9 After "after," epilogue
14 Jagged
18 *Funny Girl* actor
22 Went out
24 *Citizen Kane* estate
25 Draw out
26 Couch kin
28 Chevy SUV model
30 After "after," post meridiem
31 "My Way" songwriter
32 York symbol
36 Minnesota twins?

COZY

ACROSS

1 Like many movies nowadays
6 Bygone computer
11 New Hampshire college town
12 *Cave* ___ ("Beware of dog," in Latin)
13 Yegg
15 Sideboard
16 Like some hair: Var.
19 Lib. reference
20 *The Sixth* ___
21 ___ dish (lab item)
23 Didn't get used
24 Former Connecticut governor Ella
25 Bawl out
28 Stereo, for one
32 "___ say ..."
33 Yam, for one
34 Hip attachments?
35 Gifts on October birthdays

DOWN

1 Says "go ahead" to
2 Teachers' org.
3 Mos ___ (Jack Black's *Be Kind Rewind* costar)
4 Some sweaters
5 Dictate
6 Military sch.
7 Medieval or modern weapon
8 Tangled
9 Old dogs
10 It's hard to pick up in the mountains
14 Color of Clifford
16 1974 horror film with the tagline "Once this motion picture sinks its fangs into you, you'll never be the same"
17 Naval attire
18 Arrive without an invitation
21 Beseech
22 Thoroughly enjoys
24 Baseball VIPs
26 ___'acte
27 Hoo-has
29 Abbr. indicating an unfilled schedule slot
30 ___ roll (sushi selection)
31 "___ Robinson, you're trying to seduce me"

JACKSON 6

ACROSS

1 2000 Samuel L. Jackson film
6 2003 Samuel L. Jackson film
11 Prefix with -pathic
12 Limber
13 2000 Samuel L. Jackson film
15 Loan security
16 *Fantastic Mr. Fox* author Roald
19 Blend beforehand
23 Slugger's stat
24 Like minor home improvements, briefly
25 610, once
26 2008 Samuel L. Jackson film
28 Charon's waterway
29 Brat's look
31 2010 Samuel L. Jackson film
37 Charles and others
38 Virginia's ___ River
39 Thunderstruck
40 Creator of the Lorax, who speaks for the trees

DOWN

1 Moo ___ pork
2 Sweets
3 U.N. biggie: Abbr.
4 Wild
5 Nail holders?
6 Napoleon locale
7 Quartz variety
8 Close relative
9 "___ be!"
10 Lincoln center?
14 Headache helper
16 Court legend
17 Aladdin's sidekick
18 *Get ___ to the Greek*
20 Colo. time zone, in the summer
21 Like winter sidewalks
22 2002 Samuel L. Jackson film
24 Curtains, so to speak
27 "Fiddlesticks!"
28 Do figure eights
30 Bygone theaters
31 Prefix with lateral
32 Vote in Québec
33 Singing syllable
34 Furnace measure, for short
35 ___ *Girls* (Kelly musical)
36 Drs.' workplaces

BARE NECESSITIES

ACROSS

1 Heat to just short of boiling
6 Pat's longtime TV coworker
11 Cube root of 27
12 Perfect
13 Hotel amenity
15 Father of octuplets on *The Simpsons*
16 Laura ___ Wilder
17 Speeder's penalty
19 Haulage unit
20 Eventually become
22 Leaves a mark on
26 Ode title starter
28 March 17 slogan word
29 Galore
33 Sgt.'s mail drop
34 Councilperson
36 Take the honey and run?
37 Tarnish
38 *The Biggest* ___ (TV show)
39 Bridge declaration

DOWN

1 Attack from above
2 Penner of polonaises
3 Where the worldly-wise have been
4 Moon craft, for short
5 Lucy's hubby
6 Signs of fall
7 Forge ahead
8 Moon walker Armstrong
9 Table salt, symbolically
10 "Light" and "dark" orders
14 Treebeard, for one
18 Musical Muse
21 Think about
23 Land bordering Mesopotamia
24 Matures
25 Sty sounds
27 Dough dispenser
29 Genesis shepherd
30 Response to "Marco," at times
31 Land bordered by the Mekong
32 Abominable Snowman
35 Atlas page

STAPLES

ACROSS

1 ___ Handbook (writer's style guide)
4 Dem.'s foe
7 Amt.
10 Deserter
11 Mark of uncertainty
13 Unidentifiable cafeteria fare
15 NBA star called "The Shack"
16 *Sans* ___
17 Antithesis of Mr. Nice Guy
19 Organ parts
20 Jack
22 "Go away!"
25 It teaches freedom from desire
29 Small bands
31 Mea ___
32 Starchy sides
34 Costume in 1976's *King Kong* remake
35 Tennis court divider
36 Make one
37 Director Ang
38 Product placements

DOWN

1 Domestic comedy of '83
2 Football great Bobby whose name sounds like a country road
3 Befuddled
4 Land, as a fish
5 Blow it
6 Yields
7 File
8 Dick ___ (comics page detective)
9 Legendary mountain men
12 The Great American ___
14 Summertime shirts
18 *How to ___ Fried Worms* (classic children's book)
21 Give up
22 Scarecrow stuffing
23 ___ paper
24 Gave a hand
26 Actress Massey
27 Floor it
28 Brig's pair
30 Record store category
33 Place for a tack

BACK FLIPS

ACROSS

1 Eastern tie?
4 Sheepish sound
7 Sgt. or cpl.
10 Handled
11 Ancient greeting
12 Particular turn
13 Keyboard abbr.
14 To whom parakeets pray?
16 A bit dazed
18 "Her ___" (song from *Miss Saigon*)
19 Small swig at one end of an alley?
22 Negatively charged particle
23 Average score at an urban golf course?
28 Philosopher Descartes
29 ___ orange
30 Kidnapping rehearsal?
33 Wish
34 "___ Beso" (Paul Anka hit)
35 Deli choice
36 Foxy
37 D.C. VIP: Abbr.
38 Far-away link
39 Pipe joint

DOWN

1 Big name in brushwork?
2 Bear in *The Jungle Book*
3 Following behind
4 Mollycoddling
5 *Midnight Magic* author
6 Ireland's ___ Lingus
7 Pola of silent films
8 Walk noisily
9 Ye ___ Magick Shoppe
15 Prima ___ (divas)
17 Krypton, e.g.
20 ___ *for Noose* (Grafton book)
21 Retire
23 Where to get down?
24 Williams of *Happy Days*
25 ___ Blue Ribbon
26 Nimble
27 Color again, as gray hair
28 Numbered rds.
31 Million Mom March target: Abbr.
32 *The Fountainhead* author Rand

IMBEDDED OPPOSITES

ACROSS

1 Belief system
6 Jump out of the way
11 Spam alternative
12 Farm units
13 Cold
15 Book between Lev. and Deut.
16 Certain exercise system
17 Apple of a sort
19 Bombay Sapphire, for example
20 Coyote's genus
22 West Wing workers
26 Start of a popular round
28 Deep sleep
29 Suffered humiliation
33 It may gird a geisha
34 Good
36 *The Goat, or Who Is Sylvia?* playwright Edward
37 Golden ___ (seniors)
38 Brewing need
39 Midsection

DOWN

1 Word with food or group
2 ___ center
3 Broadway composer Jerry
4 Ref. that may fill a whole shelf
5 Train station
6 Showy bloom
7 ___ Airlines (*Lost* carrier)
8 "Nerts!"
9 Richard of *Chicago*
10 Guesses: Abbr.
14 Pudding fruit
18 Sewing groups
21 Cold dessert
23 Redecorate
24 They may flare up
25 Told it like it was
27 Bad tidings
29 On the road
30 TV part
31 Noted exile isle
32 "Come again?"
35 Many moons ___

O CAPTAIN, MY CAPTAIN!

ACROSS

1 Over again
5 Two-pointer, e.g.
11 *Little Earthquakes* singer Amos
12 Gaul invader
13 Captain ___
14 Extreme fear
15 How things may be burned?
17 Depression Era figure
18 West of Hollywood
19 Captain ___
21 Closed
23 Homes in the sticks?
27 Captain ___
29 Singer Zadora
30 German auto pioneer
33 Something that shoots spikes
35 Contemptuous looks
37 Captain ___
38 ___ *Dearest*
39 Decorative needle case
40 Having one intermission
41 Nile biters?

DOWN

1 Where a telecommuter works
2 Former Reagan speechwriter Peggy
3 Worn away
4 Online reference site, briefly
5 Sheetful of cookies
6 Gobbled (up)
7 It won't go on for long
8 Captain ___
9 *The Time Machine* race
10 Scale deduction
16 Masochist's start
20 Paul who wrote "Put Your Head on My Shoulder"
22 Skin condition
24 Malt shop choices
25 Even
26 Manhattan eatery known for its caricatures
28 Get-go
30 Cellar, in apt. ads
31 Sufficient, once
32 Captain ___
34 Crate & Barrel alternative
36 Rock's Ocasek

SEPARATION

ACROSS

1 Elemental particles
6 Like some articles: Abbr.
11 Heptad amount
12 "Nifty!"
13 With 14-Across, like some agreements
14 See 13-Across
15 Stray
16 Flock sound
18 ___ Abner
19 Kind of tide
21 How the depressed may act
23 Call it quits, and a literal hint to this puzzle's theme
25 "Begone!" of yore
27 Show about a show choir
30 Launch of 1986
31 *The Old Man and the* ___
33 Middle muscles, for short
34 With 36-Across, quill carriers
36 See 34-Across
38 French student?
39 *Falstaff* or *Fidelio*
40 Some Surrealist works
41 Daft

DOWN

1 Colorado ski town
2 Pomme de ___
3 In an awkward position
4 Door sign
5 Give the cold shoulder
6 Going nowhere?
7 Circus catcher
8 Perry White's paper
9 Online business
10 Seward's ___ (the Alaska Purchase)
17 Marble material
20 Boston skyscraper nickname, with "the"
22 National Clown Week's mo.
24 Comes after
25 Psyched
26 Cousin of a cello
28 1975 Pulitzer winner Roger
29 Opinionated work
32 Like peas in ___
35 106, long ago
37 Bus. page news

WINNING ROW

ACROSS

1 LAX org.
4 Key abbr.
7 Roman 650
10 Player with 511 career home runs
11 Impresario Ziegfeld
12 Kanga's kid
13 With 14- and 15-Across, 1995 Pearl Jam song
14 See 13-Across
15 See 13-Across
16 Hitachi competitor
18 Bad bacteria
20 *Lord of the Rings* menace
22 French accords?
23 It's often tied
27 Professor 'iggins, to Eliza
28 Try to win over
29 Some Brahms works
31 Skater Ohno
35 With 36- and 38-Across, 1987 Buster Poindexter song
36 See 35-Across
38 See 35-Across
39 U.K. record label
40 Inn order
41 I.M. Pei's alma mater
42 ___ room
43 "Theorem proved!"
44 Hostess ___ Balls

DOWN

1 A bundle
2 Athenian hub
3 Memo starter
4 Attempt
5 Traffic caution
6 Apple leftover
7 Do detox
8 Rapper Artis Ivey, familiarly
9 *Thelma &* ___
17 You might walk the dog with one
19 Residence with a board
21 Rook's call
23 Tie up
24 Where to do what the locals do
25 Judge
26 Put a layer on
30 NBA nickname
32 Units of resistance
33 A little lamb
34 Football legend Graham
37 *Fútbol* shout

BOTH SIDES NOW

ACROSS

1 Stormed
6 Manila envelope closer
11 Big name in video arcades
12 Redhead's dye
13 Tractor type
15 Dusk-___-dawn
16 Laser sound effect
17 "___ Robinson" (*The Graduate* song)
18 Ornamental attire
20 Stevenson scoundrel
22 Storied royal elephant
24 Actress Pia
27 Fill up
31 Homer's Indian friend
32 Ward workers, for short
34 Ran first
35 *A Walk in the Woods* subject
38 When Hamlet says "The play's the thing"
39 Bait, say
40 Met again
41 Spray displayers

DOWN

1 Floaters in rapids
2 Central courts
3 London lockups
4 Marine eagle
5 Airhead
6 Author Deepak
7 Place for sheep
8 "Me ___ Shadow"
9 Bergen dummy
10 Analyze, as a sentence
14 Dance craze from Brazil
19 Cable channel with Comic Relief fundraisers
21 Abbr. in a marathon time
23 Ban locale?
24 Founder of a Manhattan specialty food shop
25 Without delay
26 Tear carriers
28 Spy-fi series created by J.J. Abrams
29 Wound up
30 Borders
33 Where John Candy made his debut
36 Sephia maker
37 Mauna ___

EXTREMITIES

ACROSS

1 Big name in insurance
6 Specks
11 Belief
12 Actress Kelly
13 Lamb Chop and Judy, e.g.
15 Indie music genre
16 Splashy resort
17 Amer. soldiers
18 Arousing
20 Comic Russell
22 Warehouse
24 Casino position
27 "Darling, Je Vous ___ Beaucoup"
31 Letter carrier?: Abbr.
32 And so on: Abbr.
34 TV's *Shop ___ You Drop*
35 Treat
38 Dedicatee of a piano classic
39 Hawaiian island
40 Traffic tool
41 Clan chief of old Scotland

DOWN

1 Throbs
2 Set up
3 Big name in fine china
4 Go on to say
5 Sting participants
6 Disable
7 Alley ___
8 *The Way to Natural Beauty* author Cheryl
9 Musical Shaw
10 Flippant
14 Like the Arctic
19 Fashion inits.
21 Source of a royal pain?
23 Wobble
24 Table
25 Name on an old Boeing B-29
26 Get around
28 1986 rock autobiography
29 Where to see "The Last Supper"
30 *Watching ___* (short-lived Julia Louis-Dreyfus sitcom)
33 Bygone Briton
36 Airport screening org.
37 Cry from Ebenezer Scrooge

MIDDLE LANE

ACROSS

1 Romanov ruler
5 Honorific
10 Juan's greeting
11 Blessing preceder
12 City 70 miles north of Oklahoma City
13 Brain cell
14 ___ in apple
15 From left to right: Abbr.
16 It delivers the goods
17 "Knock it off!"
20 Mexican Revolutionary called "The Centaur of the North"
24 Cut at a slope, in Sussex
25 "His Master's Voice" label
28 Miller's lover in *Henry & June*
29 Evil
30 Shackle
32 Renounce
33 La Scala shows
34 Show subtitled *The American Tribal Love-Rock Musical*
35 Wagon alternative
36 Travel guide list

DOWN

1 Little Orphan Annie henchman
2 Beethoven's "Kreutzer ___"
3 Krauss heard on the *Cold Mountain* soundtrack
4 "Gnarly"
5 Poe classic
6 Place for preemies, in brief
7 Kind of traffic
8 Aerial maneuver
9 A long time to wait
11 Pizza topping, at times
15 Plato, for one
18 Chem. contaminant
19 Rock's ___ Tuesday
21 Mail order name
22 Segue
23 Common vipers
25 Fraternity letters
26 Deal with it
27 Like fine wines
31 ___ la la
32 "The Sweetheart of Sigma ___"

RISE AND FALL

ACROSS

1 Magnate
6 Old anesthetic
11 Dean Martin song subject
12 Arrowsmith's wife
13 1967 5th Dimension song
15 Engraved letters?
16 Like sandals
17 Client
19 Dr. ___
20 Bunch of papers
22 Maudlin
26 Pulitzer-winning writer Robertson
28 Word before market or circus
29 One hitting "send"
33 The Trojans of the NCAA
34 Peter Gabriel song from *Wall-E*
36 Govt. security
37 Praise
38 Reason to receive a medal, perhaps
39 Orders to go?

DOWN

1 Ford debut of 1988
2 Spritely, say
3 Rug
4 Contemporary of Duchamp
5 In apple-pie order
6 Respected ones
7 It may be read
8 British general who captured New York City in 1776
9 Times to live through
10 They may be cosmic
14 Go-ahead sign
18 Encountered by coincidence
21 Bumble
23 Like mice and geese
24 Pounding tool that goes with a mortar
25 Craft for the wealthy
27 Modern: Prefix
29 1999 Ron Howard film
30 ___ *Lisa Smile*
31 Likely to be chased by MPs
32 It may be blowing in the wind
35 Firefighting tool

VOWEL PLAY

ACROSS

1 Noodles
6 Sinclair who wrote *The Jungle*
11 Equipment for a modern pentathlon
12 ___ jacket
13 Breathing room
14 Going rate
15 Dutch carrier
16 Gray, in a way
18 Howard of comedy
19 Polite response
21 Break
23 Coward's lack
25 Like fraudulent accidents
28 Edvard Munch Museum locale
32 Feel awful
33 Cause of Cleopatra's demise
35 Roadside jumpers: Abbr.
36 Chex carrier
38 Grit
40 Gandhi, e.g.
41 Moses's mount
42 Frequent Woody Allen theme
43 Pick on

DOWN

1 Annoying, as a gnat
2 Bobbing object
3 Dress lines
4 Clue collector, slangily
5 In full sail
6 Invisible
7 Get-up-and-go
8 Composer's basis
9 Double Stuf cookies, e.g.
10 *David* and others
17 Diagrams
20 N.Y. Knicks venue
22 Bill Gates, e.g.: Abbr.
24 Mr. ___
25 Barack's youngest
26 Easy two-pointer
27 *Merrily We Roll ___* (Sondheim show that goes backward in time)
29 Spa spot
30 Turner and others
31 Actor Jack of *The Great Dictator*
34 "Hey, there!"
37 Some EMT cases
39 Mincemeat dessert

LOOK BOTH WAYS

ACROSS

1 Bus driver on *The Simpsons* (#1)
5 Landing locale
11 Like some thermometers
12 Food brand named after two states
13 Introduction to the first lady? (#2)
15 Desert drainage basin
16 New York Shakespeare Festival founder
17 Owns
18 "The best policy"
21 What stealth planes avoid (#3)
22 Sporting a tag
25 Ref. work
28 "___ Lang Syne"
29 Middle of many Grafton titles
31 Words from one who wants some sound equipment? (#4)
34 Fix, as a pump
35 Calls to toreadors
36 Hoffman of films
37 *The Mikado* role ___-Bo (#5)

DOWN

1 That certain "something"
2 Bit of a merry refrain
3 Unveiling shouts
4 Famous name in oil
5 You, to Yves
6 Usher's offering
7 Grim one?
8 Guy with a special touch
9 Make fit
10 Like some humor
14 Palace, in Hindi
19 "___ to the West Wind"
20 Comaneci of gymnastics
21 In great demand
22 Scot with a lot
23 Pot-___ (French stew)
24 Seventh heaven
25 Use TurboTax, say
26 Like some bank checking
27 Not stale, as chips
30 Get the goods
32 Champion of 10/30/74
33 Place to hibernate

FLYING COLORS

ACROSS

1 Wanderers
6 Iffy response
11 Get the lead out?
12 Dunkable treats
13 False leads
15 Ride, so to speak
16 Carry-on checkers: Abbr.
18 Tour de France distances
22 New York city
25 Show of lights
26 Dedicated verse
27 Rocker Ted
30 Edits
35 Shot
36 Chekhov's *Uncle ___*
37 They may pass in the night
38 Comic Bob who appeared in *The Aristocrats*

DOWN

1 One of LBJ's beagles
2 Nickel in a pocket, say?
3 ___ day
4 Workplace watchdog org.
5 Visionary
6 Choice bit
7 Aretha's record label after Atlantic
8 Craving
9 Wetlands area
10 Tricky curve
14 Arcade classic in which you could be a giant lizard, a giant ape, or a giant werewolf
16 Its hub was in St. Louis
17 Moo ___ pork
19 Civil unrest
20 Finish
21 Wind dir.
23 Get in shape
24 Flies off the handle
28 Ltr. holders
29 Final Four gp.
30 Religious sects.?
31 "Well, ___-di-dah!"
32 Wire service inits.
33 Common name for sodium hydroxide
34 Was on one's rocker, say

VACATION PLANS

ACROSS

1 Heavy blow
5 Timespan with a nickname, maybe
11 Vision: Prefix
12 Lined up
13 B-side of "Jailhouse Rock"
15 Nomadic mob
16 Fair ___ (Civil War battle site)
17 Charleson of *Chariots of Fire*
18 Salt, chemically
21 Pesticide applier
26 Singer McEntire
27 "Hooray!"
28 "The Big One," briefly
31 "The Best ___ to Come"
33 Working closely together
36 Jessica in *Murder, She Wrote*
37 Iowa State locale
38 Like a pittance
39 ___ *One* (Rufus Wainwright CD)

DOWN

1 *American ___* (classic painting)
2 Big commotion
3 Buffet table heater
4 ___ the Wet Sprocket
5 Not so bright
6 Suffix with ethyl
7 ___ oil
8 Opera highlight
9 Pier
10 Ones herded by Babe
14 Needing kneading
19 Police dept. alert
20 Online "List" creator Newmark
22 Certain feline families
23 Cellist heard with Bobby McFerrin on the album *Hush*
24 Value of an ace, at times
25 Makeup exam
28 "Wake Me Up Before You Go-Go" group
29 Flag
30 Swenson of *Benson*
32 Common KFC side
34 Not feeling 100%
35 Vote from a con

ROYAL WE

ACROSS

1 Hero's list
6 The end
11 Xenophile's friend
12 Wanderer
13 Royal flush member, maybe
15 Dangerous partner
16 Beer, sometimes
19 It's a long story
23 Sculler
24 Defense org. until 1992
26 "C'mon, ___ pal!"
27 Public pool place, perhaps
29 Yo-yo brand
31 Dangerous, colloquially
33 Leona Helmsley's royal nickname, with "the"
39 October handout
40 Printer brand
41 Orange covers
42 Intact

DOWN

1 U.S. terr., 1861–89
2 Inventor Whitney
3 Richard Strauss's ___ Heldenleben
4 L'Absinthe painter
5 Big bores, slangily
6 First word of "The Raven"
7 Like stuff in the back of the fridge, maybe
8 Ostrich's cousin
9 Chat
10 Print ___
14 Its range is 88–108 MHz
16 Coquettish
17 ___ and Swiss
18 Circle segment
20 Easy threesome?
21 Peggy of The Dukes of Hazzard
22 Bert's fictional twin sister
25 A time to remember?
28 Coming up
30 Insect stage
32 Hill group
33 Fiscal per.
34 Geller with paranormal claims
35 Poet's period after dusk
36 That, south of the border
37 Yahoo! competitor
38 Phoenix-to-Flagstaff dir.

TWO CANS

ACROSS

1 Upright
6 Actor Willie of *Eight Is Enough*
11 Serta rival
12 "Fantastic!"
13 Two cans
15 Game you can't play left-handed
16 "Save me!," e.g.
19 Neckwear option
24 Orbach with a recurring role on *Murder, She Wrote*
26 Quarterback attack
27 A bit
29 In ___ of
30 Marcel Marceau, e.g.
32 Two cans
39 "Talk turkey," e.g.
40 Match, in grammar
41 Heaven-sent food
42 Mike seen in the ring

DOWN

1 Curvy path
2 Not opt.
3 ___ de cologne
4 Ready-made graphics
5 Rookie
6 Soak up
7 Noted Zurich artist
8 Disfigure
9 Perón of Argentina
10 Sauce source
14 Mom's specialty, briefly
16 What to wear while out?
17 MGM lion's name
18 Act human?
20 Zicam target
21 Numeral in a Uris title
22 Filled the bill?
23 Lao-___
25 Subject of an insult, perhaps
28 Tailoring job
31 Butcher's goods
32 Duncan of the NBA
33 Lupino of *High Sierra*
34 *Ladders to Fire* writer Anaïs
35 Triumphed
36 It has a variety of schedules: Abbr.
37 Prefix with conservative
38 Col.'s boss

BEATLEMANIA

ACROSS

1 Italian alternative
6 Mazda competitor
11 "What a kidder!"
12 Barbarian of pulp tales
13 Pee-wee Herman's real name
15 Inuit: Abbr.
16 Med. orders
17 Early Beatle Sutcliffe
18 "The Raven" poet's monogram
19 Take an electronic picture of
20 Largest signature on the Declaration of Indepedence
24 Poet Juana ___ de la Cruz
25 Rapa ___ (Easter Island)
26 Neighbor of Aus.
27 Credo
28 *Face/Off* director John
31 Costar of Walter Matthau in *The Sunshine Boys*
34 Telling tales
35 Sports equipment used with masks
36 Tiny
37 1964 Lorne Greene song about a gunfighter

DOWN

1 Hitchcock flick
2 Cries of discovery
3 Curly cue?
4 Maj.'s superior
5 Cry of triumph
6 People are closely watched in them: Abbr.
7 Melodramatic outburst
8 Intl. cultural org.
9 Pepcid alternative
10 Still afloat
14 Sweep
18 Dash widths
19 Grade sch. subj.
20 Move like Jell-O
21 Jack of hearts trait
22 Junk, so to speak
23 Cabaret selection
27 Rocker ___ Pop
28 Birdhouse bird
29 Blood type, briefly
30 ___ buco
32 Shot putters?: Abbr.
33 News inits.

DOUBLE STANDARD

ACROSS

1 Foxes
8 Certain visitors from far away, briefly
11 Blah
12 Magnum, e.g.: Abbr.
13 "Where the West Begins"
14 ___ canal
15 ___ Canals
16 Inferior
18 Trojan War hero
21 Flashes in the pan, musically
24 Droning, as a voice
25 Patti LuPone title role
26 Uncouth one
29 Triangle part
30 Comforting words
34 Word after American or slippery
35 Henry II's queen
36 JFK gp.
37 "Go away!"

DOWN

1 Coppertone nos.
2 Suffix with switch
3 Preliminary tic-tac-toe question
4 Sixth-generation video game system, briefly
5 Bowman's need
6 "___-Willow" (*The Mikado* song)
7 Classic brand of bike
8 Channel swimmer Gertrude
9 Promo
10 Emphasize
17 Antique, once
18 *Cat on ___ Tin Roof*
19 Stronghold
20 Pipe contents
21 Egg dish
22 Steel works?
23 Stumper
26 "Rule, Britannia" composer
27 "No ___!"
28 Orphan of literature
31 Córdoba cheer
32 Butterfly catcher's need
33 Bar-closing time, maybe

MIXED METAPHOR

ACROSS

1 "Um ..."
5 Soft drink brand
11 Prefix with logical
12 Stewed
13 Filberts and cashews
14 Actress Plummer
15 Tool for terrestrial cleaning?
17 Great ___
18 "Spare me the details," in textspeak
21 Extension
22 Atkinson of *Mr. Bean*
24 ___ *v. Wade*
25 They blow off steam
27 Where to shop for new dreams?
28 6"×9" book size
31 "___ From Muskogee"
32 Double flat?
33 Trickle (through)
34 ___ *Rides Again* (1939 western)
35 Hall and Roush

DOWN

1 Place for a Pinot
2 The Blair Witch Project codirector Sánchez
3 Not make an issue of
4 Was beaten by
5 Eastern mystic
6 Deli order
7 "Pronto!"
8 Depot: Abbr.
9 Actor Danson
10 Orthodontists' org.
16 2009 Todd Phillips film, with *The*
18 Fine-tuned
19 Not single
20 Sock sections
23 Undergo diffusion
26 Strong glue
27 Shut down
28 Uneven
29 Pool stick
30 Does some vandalizing, briefly

SENSE OF DIRECTION

ACROSS

1 Math course, briefly
5 Pyle player
11 State where *Glee* and *The Drew Carey Show* are set
12 Recipe amount
13 Electrical units
14 Go back on a vow
15 Vampire of fiction
17 Do needlework
18 Unhealthy-looking
20 Holman who was known as Mr. Basketball
21 Needle point
23 Needle point
25 Computer family member
26 *Out of Africa* name
28 Do needlework
30 God of fertility
34 ___ of (rather than)
36 Computer clickers
37 Christie sleuth
38 Bingo call
39 Nike logo
40 Stable diet?

DOWN

1 Fuel from a mine
2 "Sigh ..."
3 "Loose ___ sink ships"
4 Sportscaster Bob
5 Needle point
6 Hydrocarbon ending
7 Make curves
8 Oodles
9 Baby, slangily
10 Exhausted
16 Vino region
19 First group to vote
21 Sift
22 Estevez of *Men at Work*
24 Out-elbowed?
25 Record problems
27 Needle point
29 Rookie: Var.
31 Actress Hayworth
32 Tracy Marrow, familiarly
33 Capitol Hill figures: Abbr.
35 Dawn goddess

KIDS!

ACROSS

1 "Spare me the details," initially
4 Teeming group
7 Be in bed, maybe
10 "___ the Walrus"
11 Police sheet letters
12 Weeding tool
13 Handheld organizer, briefly
14 Ice machine
16 Musical that won four Tony Awards in 2006
18 Yemeni capital
19 Sermon subject
20 Indian flatbread
21 Product of Sweden
25 One in favor
28 Equipped
29 Musical that won six Tony Awards in 1982
32 Escapist?
33 DHL alternative
34 Top or bottom
35 Part of RSVP
36 Opposite of post-
37 Retainer, e.g.
38 Future citizen's course: Abbr.
39 How-___ (tutorials)

DOWN

1 It may be beside a register
2 Got along
3 Turkish inn
4 Challenge for a rat
5 Initials
6 Buck of filmdom
7 Salty salutation
8 Cyclotron bits
9 Wreath
15 Potted tree
17 Attacked in a sneaky manner
22 Sudden
23 Football star's title
24 *I've Got a Secret* panelist Myerson and first lady Truman
26 Poker ploy
27 Onetime Dodges
29 Completed
30 Obnoxious
31 Willem Dafoe's *Finding Nemo* role
32 Bunny boss, briefly

RESTAURANT NO-NO'S

ACROSS

1 Audition tapes
6 City once called Philadelphia
11 The Oregon Trail crossed it
12 Prefix with linguistics
13 Gym wear for a bench presser
15 Lies
16 Just know
19 Camp sights, for short
22 Footwear for a bobbysoxer
25 Initials at sea
26 Horseshoes score
27 Bicuspid neighbor
29 Vacationer's delivery option
35 Prepare (oneself)
36 Coppers
37 Sculpture subject
38 Dynamic start?

DOWN

1 Barely lit
2 URL ending
3 More, in Managua
4 "Rats!"
5 Cirque du ___
6 Gal Friday: Abbr.
7 Mineral hardness scale inventor
8 1,101
9 Subject of EPA monitoring
10 Word with waste and want
14 Actress Getty
16 Bear or bull suffix
17 *Coming Home* subject, briefly
18 Gridders' scores: Abbr.
19 *Apollo 13* director Howard
20 Churchillian sign
21 Lith., formerly
23 One may be warranted
24 Jimmy Stewart movie
27 Strasbourg ladies: Abbr.
28 Norwegian capital
29 Q-U connection
30 Platte Valley native
31 Word in "The Star-Spangled Banner"
32 Swing voter, perhaps: Abbr.
33 Nexus: Abbr.
34 "¿Cómo es ___?" ("How come?")

PAIR OF SOX

ACROSS

1 Mussolini's ideology
8 Telephonic 3
11 Peach Bowl venue
12 The self-proclaimed "Greatest"
13 Threw some cereal out of a club?
15 *Caddyshack* director
16 Search (into)
17 AOL and such
18 Barn sound
19 Coupon amt.
20 Quick sidestep
21 Omaha beach craft: Abbr.
24 Dow Jones paper, for short
25 Feature of an old-fashioned roast
26 Secret society
29 Hispaniola half
30 Gulp down underworld river water?
32 Word on all U.S. coins
33 *Amadeus* antagonist
34 ___-pitch softball
35 Put down

DOWN

1 Chiffon, for one
2 Reception shout
3 Declines
4 ___ Major
5 Business abbrs.
6 Sault ___ Marie
7 Ripple alternative
8 *James and the Giant Peach* author
9 Mountain stat.
10 Set, in Somme
14 Corp. biggie
18 Rank below Lt. Col.
20 Gabor born Sári
21 Stick around
22 Lecherous goat-men
23 Ed's wife on *The Honeymooners*
24 Richard Pryor title role, with "the"
25 Count in music
26 E-mail: Abbr.
27 MP's quarry
28 Pooch handle. stereotypically
29 Beatles hit of 1965
31 Vegas opener

NOT LYING

ACROSS

1 Tore
6 Rambo-esque
11 Escape from
12 Not listed above
13 Watching the wee ones
15 Thurman of *My Super Ex-Girlfriend*
16 "Good night, sweet ladies. Good night, good night" speaker
17 It has several movements
19 Taken in
20 Breakfast item
22 Noted initials in sketch comedy
25 Academy graduate
29 Platitudes
31 MIV halved
32 "Excellent!"
34 Retort in a playground argument
35 Napping
36 Happy sound
37 Attar source

DOWN

1 *Concentration* puzzle
2 San Antonio landmark
3 Like some cigars
4 Dreyer's partner in ice cream
5 Firedome, for example
6 Hole maker
7 Bears witness, with "to"
8 Easter Island's owner
9 *Iceland* star Sonja
10 Radio City Music Hall fixture
14 Locale in a 1964 hit
18 One who does some counseling
21 Open with a click
22 Hardly the screaming type
23 Pulverize
24 Full chorus, in music
26 Pinhead
27 Tokyo shopping district
28 Actor Bruce of radio's *Sherlock Holmes*
30 Depot
33 WWII gen.

COMEDY DUO

ACROSS

1 Covalent bond formers
6 They branch off
11 Lunar "seas"
12 Accumulate
13 Peels out
15 More loved
16 Word before free or bound
19 Goiter treatment
22 Poultry that tastes like beef
23 "This is ___"
24 Accomplished
25 Toper's total
27 Hot
28 Frog's place?
30 Tool that turns a hexagonal screw
35 "If My Friends Could ___ Now"
36 *The Sound of Music* girl who isn't Liesl, Louisa, Brigitta, or Gretl
37 Parker in *Waiting for Guffman*
38 Like a whip?

DOWN

1 U.N. figure: Abbr.
2 Fraternity "T"
3 Bobby of hockey
4 '70s–'80s sitcom title role
5 Writer's Market abbr.
6 Bad guy in *The Lord of the Rings*
7 Fix firmly in place
8 Trip to the airport, say
9 *Cats* monogram
10 Old geographical inits.
14 Symbol of pride?
16 Belle of the ball
17 Cécile portrayer in *Dangerous Liaisons*
18 Chocolate treats
20 Countermand
21 B movie actress Williams
23 1974 Oscar winner
26 Word before park or song
27 It may be let off
29 Uzis and AK-47's
30 Hooded menace
31 Son in *The Little Foxes*
32 Gun owners' gp.
33 Gathering place: Abbr.
34 It's sometimes passed

RE: PETE

ACROSS

1 *So Long, and Thanks for All the Fish* author Douglas
6 Chrysler make
11 Solicits, with "up"
12 Type type
13 Places for American Beauties
15 Pained shouts
16 U2 guitarist
17 Goddess pictured in Egyptian tombs
19 Gp. with a staff in its symbol
20 Bursts (with)
22 Rice who wrote *Street Scene*
26 Have something
28 ___-Am (Dr. Seuss character)
29 Not at all calm
33 Carson City's st.
34 Oscar category
36 Rathbone who played Sherlock Holmes
37 Carrier name until 1997
38 *Calendrier* span
39 Has a wearying effect

DOWN

1 Deft
2 Nod off
3 Bush dweller, maybe
4 Abbr. on a French letter
5 Army NCO
6 "You don't think I'd do it, do you?"
7 Trials
8 Went "pffft"
9 Thieves' group
10 "So what ___ is new?"
14 "I found it!"
18 Necco wafer alternative
21 Like child's play
23 Car owner's reference
24 TV chef Lagasse
25 Kansas and Kentucky
27 *South Pacific* prop
29 "Does Your Mother Know" singers
30 Be less than level
31 Abbr. in many group names
32 Bra specification
35 Airport org.

DICHOTOMY

ACROSS

1 Minute part
5 Grilled dishes
11 Panty raid site
12 Puts in office
13 Like some cases
15 Japanese sneakers?
16 Sloppy kiss
18 Proceed without the words
21 Sides in debates
24 Beatnik's exclamation
25 Big name in antivirus software
26 Like sour grapes
28 Good-natured exchange
33 How some slogans are delivered
34 Turner and others
35 Teatime pastries
36 Like some important mail: Abbr.

DOWN

1 "If ___ say so myself"
2 Alley of Moo
3 Capital on the Delaware
4 Procedures performed by OBs
5 *Brainiac* author
6 Alan of *Manhattan Murder Mystery*
7 "I Loves You, Porgy" singer
8 Gaelic "Gee!"
9 Air conditioner measure, for short
10 Plane with a tipped nose
14 *V* villainess played by Morena Baccarin
16 Typing stat.
17 Historic period
18 Big seller, proverbially
19 Classic card game
20 Co. with a butterfly logo
22 Jimmy of *The Mickey Mouse Club*
23 Backseat driver, e.g.
26 ___ *Flux* (2005 Charlize Theron film)
27 Sugar source
28 Mil. workers
29 Ltd., in the States
30 Brandy bottle ltrs.
31 Plunk prefix
32 Body shop fig.

PLUSH

ACROSS

1 Pointer, perhaps
6 Sporty sunroof
10 Merge
11 Christine of *Chicago Hope*
12 First-aid tent?
14 Fighting words
15 Big stinger
18 Like a B'way hit
21 Four-letter words from Friends?
24 ___City (classic computer game that launched a series)
25 "___ can eat!"
26 Badly bruised
29 Cue from the uncoifed?
34 Become accustomed (to)
35 Muse of love poetry
36 Reproduce
37 Is apparently

DOWN

1 Thought was really cool
2 "___ pig's eye!"
3 Dog-tag wearers, briefly
4 Opinion leader?
5 Guinea pig, in a way
6 "See ya!"
7 Parched
8 Siouan speaker
9 ATM card necessity
11 "I Fought the ___"
13 Women's shoe fasteners
15 CO's hangouts
16 Word repeated before "Marie" in a 1918 song title
17 Builds, as excitement
19 P
20 The Buckeyes: Abbr.
22 Skateboarding moves
23 Porto ___, Brazil
27 *Driving Miss Daisy* playwright
28 Ham holder, often
29 Disposable pen maker
30 One for Juan
31 Glaswegian denial
32 20s dispenser
33 ___ Alamos

BROKEN PROMISES

ACROSS

1 Bellhop's burden
4 Tiny lie
7 Et ___ (and the following): Abbr.
10 Santa ___ winds
11 Comedian Philips
12 Capote, to friends
13 "23 ___!"
14 *Lady ___ Train* (1945 film)
15 Wonderland cake words
17 Up ___
19 Rose of rock
21 Common sorbet container size
22 "Big Papi"
26 Home of Organ Pipe Cactus Natl. Mon.
27 Diet-based meas.
28 Old radio's Fibber ___
30 Abu ___
34 ___ Paulo
35 Small screen star
37 Baseball Hall of Famer Roush
38 Something to pick
39 Ques. response
40 Site of some gamboling
41 Sedaris of *Strangers With Candy*
42 Start of an apology

DOWN

1 Slider's goal
2 "(You're) Having My Baby" songwriter
3 Trot or canter, e.g.
4 Send, in a way
5 "As I see it," online
6 Bounce
7 "That's enough!"
8 1844 Verdi work
9 Hard rock
16 Mayan staple
18 *The Color Purple* actress, familiarly
20 One in charge: Abbr.
22 Woman in distress?
23 Game keeper?
24 Abe of *Barney Miller*
25 Curious thing
29 Pittsburgh suburb
31 ___ West of *Family Guy*
32 Hammer or anvil, e.g.
33 Rick's *Casablanca* love
36 Energy

KVETCH ME IF YOU CAN

ACROSS

1 23-/25-Across film
6 Prosciutto
9 Conquest of 1953
12 Old White House nickname
13 23-/25-Across film
14 *Mad ___* (Mel Gibson film)
15 Pontiac classics
17 Passé
20 Panamanian dictator of the '80s
23 With 25-Across, this puzzle's subject
25 See 23-Across
26 Crush, e.g.
28 Word after fruit or horse
29 Hot rum mixture
30 Purchase for a disguise
32 23-/25-Across film
38 Unsettle
39 Most minimally worded
40 Call at sea, maybe
41 23-/25-Across film

DOWN

1 Grandpa on *The Waltons*
2 ___ Marie Saint
3 Novelist Deighton
4 Recipient of yearly contributions
5 Four-star officer: Abbr.
6 23-/25-Across role, sometimes
7 FBI list letters
8 Vicente Fox's country: Abbr.
10 Starch tree
11 Woman's shoe
16 Masseur's supply
17 Punch lines?
18 Place for a pit stop in London
19 California team
20 Big Apple paper, in brief
21 Toothpaste type
22 "___ Day Now" (1962 hit)
24 Org. since 1890
27 Gawk at
30 Spinners, briefly
31 Ming of the NBA
33 Detergent brand
34 Night school course: Abbr.
35 Louvre Pyramid architect
36 Top-left PC key
37 Mailman's path: Abbr.

71

BACK FORMATION

ACROSS

1 Gives an edge to
6 Strollers, in England
11 Battery terminal
12 Mandel of *St. Elsewhere*
13 Comedy legend
15 Comedy bit
16 X, sometimes
17 "I'm so glad!"
18 Frequent statement in a long-distance relationship
21 Ill-fated German admiral
22 Alien on *The Simpsons*
26 "Anything you say"
30 Langley, for one: Abbr.
33 "I love," in Latin
34 Author Umberto
35 Facial features
38 Mel who voiced many cartoon characters
39 Cathedral features
40 To whom the Kaaba is dedicated
41 Shoe material

DOWN

1 Traditional Scottish dish
2 Highway entry
3 Knuckle rub
4 E-mail address ending
5 Religious factions
6 Device for LPs
7 Neighbor of Bulgaria: Abbr.
8 "Come Sail ___" (Styx song)
9 Actress Sorvino
10 Titillating
14 "Yo!"
19 Put in stitches
20 Plucked instrument
23 Unwilling (to)
24 Made out
25 ___ *Pointe Blank*
27 Devise, as a plot
28 Poehler of *Parks and Recreation*
29 ___ de Torquemada
30 "Take a Chance on Me" group
31 Collapsed
32 Jezebel's idol
36 Actress Merkel
37 Manjula's husband on *The Simpsons*

B&N

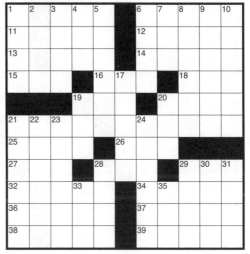

ACROSS

1 Volkswagen model
6 Actress Marisa
11 Perfection itself
12 1936 Olympics star Jesse
13 Picker's need
14 Former Cincinnati Reds catcher
15 RN's colleague
16 Dumfries denial
18 Half an exchange
19 Clairvoyance
20 Comic Carvey
21 Site of some legalized gambling
25 Scrambled wd.
26 Whopper
27 It's south of Eur.
28 Nice attraction
29 W-2 info
32 Hand drum
34 Con game
36 Operatic tunes
37 Had a homemade meal
38 Stock up
39 Birds in a V formation, often

DOWN

1 Be in harmony (with)
2 North Holland seaport
3 Piece of camping equipment
4 ___ Mahal
5 King of Naples in *The Tempest*
6 *Hamlet* soliloquy starter
7 Be in debt
8 ___ telepathy
9 San Fernando Valley community
10 Famed film flop
17 Tree in the Garden of the Hesperides
19 Frangipane ingredient
20 Dr. of rap
21 Nursery rhyme start
22 Tip off
23 Land reached via a wardrobe
24 Crash cushioner
28 Model Kate
29 Old knife
30 Slope needs
31 How many symphonies Chopin wrote
33 It may be natural
35 Colorado Indian

STAGE BRACKET

ACROSS

1 "Fie, I say!"
4 American ___
7 L.A. sked abbr.
10 "___ before beauty"
11 "She loves me ___"
12 Where Lux. is
13 23-Across in which the word "robot" was coined
14 21-/23-Across of 1965
15 23-Across that won a Tony and an Emmy for its star
16 Piggy's love
18 Sticks around a game parlor
19 Attacks
21 Top
23 Stage show
24 Discuss one's trade with a coworker
26 Kimono closers
27 Arbitrary parental explanation
31 23-Across that won the 1999 Pulitzer Prize
32 21-/23-Across of 1998
33 21-/23-Across of 2010

34 Shoebox letters
35 Brooks of *The Producers*
36 Commanded
37 Pts. of forks
38 Keats's "___ to Psyche"
39 Dash meas.

DOWN

1 Intruder alert?
2 Fluish feeling
3 Frankfurter, maybe
4 Signs up for a tour
5 Boors
6 "I want my ___!" ('80s slogan)

7 First name in 1960s pop
8 Certain thing
9 Bridge support
17 Disguises
18 Part of an apology
20 Last Supper guest
21 Pampered
22 Upper crusts
24 Castle turret
25 Brought on board
28 Every 12 mos.
29 One of many on a strawberry
30 *Against All ___*
32 Some Latin, for lovers

DOUBLE STAR

ACROSS

1 Sylvester Stallone film
6 Sylvester Stallone film
11 Concert venue
12 Rome's home
13 Slobber
14 Caravel features
15 Some "Angels"
17 James Caan film
20 Fleming and McKellen
23 "Who, me?"
24 "Oh yeah? ___ who?"
26 World of ___ (computer game)
27 Banks on the runway
29 James Caan film
31 Time to quit?
33 "___ to Kill For" (*Sin City* story)
35 One-eyed *Futurama* female
39 Sleep disrupter, maybe
40 Joyce Carol ___
41 Sandra Bullock film
42 Sandra Bullock film

DOWN

1 "Awesome!"
2 1967 NHL Rookie of the Year
3 Business bigwig
4 Radio features
5 Some Ivy grads
6 Frost, to a poet
7 Early name in home computers
8 Hands-on experience?
9 Deli sandwich
10 Sounds of woe
16 Krispy ___ doughnuts
17 CPR expert
18 "Blue Bayou" singer Orbison
19 American charge
21 Postal motto conjunction
22 Tofu base
25 Freezer bag brand
28 *@#%&*! Smilers* singer Mann
30 Campaign tactic
32 Sell
33 Donkey
34 Quick swim
36 O'Hare data: Abbr.
37 ___ *Liaisons Dangereuses*
38 Cigarette residue

"GEEZ!"

ACROSS

1 Breakfast options
6 Waterlogged
11 Surgery aid
12 "I love you," *en español*
13 "Tomorrow People" singer
15 Masthead figs.
16 Key grip workplace
17 Musician Brian
18 Cat call?
20 Mother's *hermana*
22 Moore costar
24 Hot trend
28 TV tycoon Turner
30 "The wolf ___ the door"
31 Singer Sumac
34 Slice
36 Fast food chain
37 1969's Best Actress
40 Zagreb native
41 Corbin's *L.A. Law* role
42 Texas A&M athlete
43 Bobby who lost to Billie Jean

DOWN

1 Dermatologist's diagnosis, maybe
2 Emulates a flying squirrel
3 Has trouble swallowing
4 Online "Holy cow!"
5 1974 Gould/ Sutherland spoof
6 Unwanted noise
7 "___ the ramparts ..."
8 Forceful wind
9 Some gangbusters
10 Stringed toy
14 Mr. ___ (Citi Field mascot)
19 In need of a change, perhaps
21 Uris hero ___ Ben Canaan
23 Enumerate
25 Making inquiries
26 Rubenesque
27 Emulates Goya
29 Directly, directionally
31 Where basketball and volleyball were first played
32 Actress Helgenberger
33 Wide-eyed
35 Nicholas I, e.g.
38 Moo goo ___ pan
39 Scanner, for short

SCRAMBLED YEGG

ACROSS

1 Hand, in 12-Across
5 Blue ___ (likely liberal)
11 *Sin City* actress Jessica
12 *Guys and Dolls* setting
13 Official at a potato bag competition?
15 Mower maker
16 With 24-Across, rare sideshow attraction?
19 Cockney abodes
23 Tiptop
24 See 16-Across
25 ___ pole
27 Martini's partner
28 Pal for Pierre
30 Penn, e.g.: Abbr.
31 Yegg (and anagram of the shaded answers)
36 Don of *Heaven Can Wait*
37 Engage
38 Cascades pk.
39 Hot spot in Italy

DOWN

1 Some household heads
2 Carte starter
3 David Sarnoff's creation of 1926
4 Symbol of strength
5 Don't be a hog
6 Snack in a hard or soft shell
7 NYC's Fifth, e.g.
8 Sea salt
9 Route abbr.
10 U.K. fliers
14 Fabled creature
16 Was on a jury
17 Dove call
18 Army unit?
19 Treasure on the Spanish Main
20 Military set of utensils
21 Part of E.T.
22 Colorado's Snowmass, e.g.
24 Cold, *en español*
26 Virile
29 Subject of the lyric "A horse is a horse, of course, of course"
31 Friend of Frodo
32 Invoice fig.
33 Yiddish "Yuck!"
34 Prefix with sphere
35 *Evita* narrator

DOMESTIC RELATIONS

ACROSS

1 Pirate's supporter, perhaps
7 Ballad, often
11 Vocal passage
12 It means "red" in Mongolian
13 *Rosencrantz and Guildenstern Are Dead* playwright
15 Angry, with "up"
16 Supplies, as assistance
17 Freezer stuff
18 *The King and I* star Brynner
19 Game of evasion, which is also a hint to this puzzle's theme
25 Bits of advice
26 Former Serbian capital
27 Treble clef readers
30 Time on the job
32 Dead head?
34 In a bit
35 Most cunning
36 Curtain inserts
37 Charge for cash

DOWN

1 *Sleepers* costar Jason
2 Beethoven symphony
3 Vodka cocktail
4 Get checkmated
5 Founded: Abbr.
6 Baby talk syllable
7 Elvis's birthplace
8 King of comedy
9 Cooking fat
10 Loose ___
14 Jack Horner's find
18 Bowl stats: Abbr.
20 Decorates
21 Looking for dirt, perhaps
22 Org. that won the 1965 Peace Prize
23 Gary of *Apollo 13*
24 Will matter
27 A bit cracked
28 *If Roast Beef Could Fly* author Jay
29 Plodded
30 Preserve, in a way
31 Barber's job
33 Govt. construction overseer

THE "IN" CROWD

ACROSS

1 Join a queue, literally
8 Homes on wheels, briefly
11 ___ *Greatest Hits* (1971 collection)
12 Suffix with malt- or lact-
13 Made a claim early
14 Urge to attack, with "on"
15 Blog feed abbr.
16 Livestock feed
18 Keep aware of, literally
19 Choral part
22 Wall Street table heading: Abbr.
23 Words of contingency, literally
27 The Kennedy years, figuratively
28 %: Abbr.
31 Motor add-on?
32 Circuit well-trod by Bob Hope
34 Kenny G's instrument
35 Confiscation
36 What an assessor assesses
37 Divide evenly, literally

DOWN

1 Bert who sang "If I Were King of the Forest"
2 Savings plans
3 Night sch. achievements
4 Flight board listing: Abbr.
5 2003 Nick Lachey hit "___ Swear"
6 Fat cat
7 *Ah, Wilderness!* mother
8 Nun's set of beads
9 Gestures from love-in participants
10 Break away
17 Country way
18 Grimace
19 Solicit aggressively
20 Yellow Teletubby
21 Discount clothing chain
24 Half-melted snow
25 Out ___ (cruising)
26 Zeno, notably
28 Grimace
29 Hair roller result
30 Not kosher
33 Lao-___

FILLING STATION

ACROSS

1 Hosp. workers
4 Gym unit
7 Computer program, informally
10 Ooh and ___
11 Pierre's friend
12 Coif holder
13 Word with wedding
15 Like very narrow shoes
16 Whole lot
17 Cereal brand
19 Fanatical
22 Old-school diaper fastener
24 Audience member, for one
25 Comics dog
26 Go kaput, with "out"
30 Sportage maker
31 "___ Candles"
34 Game show VIP's
35 Summer, on the Seine
36 "As I see it," to a textpert
37 ___ out a living
38 They may be real or imaginary: Abbr.
39 Bagel store offering

DOWN

1 Father's offering
2 Willy Wonka creator
3 Clog, e.g.
4 Joplin piece
5 Grounded bird
6 Contagious conjuctivitis
7 He's won all four Grand Slam titles
8 Female fowl
9 Tartan pattern
14 Half-price ticket
18 Facet
20 Lloyd who debated Quayle in 1988
21 Benchmark: Abbr.
22 Gift giver, briefly
23 Not troubled
24 1964 Elvis song
27 Trompe l'___
28 Captain played in film by James Mason
29 Fort ___ (gold site)
32 Skating champion Midori
33 Marks, as a ballot

MANAGED CARES

ACROSS

1 Mule of old song
4 "Suzie Q" band, briefly
7 "Little" '60s singer
10 Air quality org.
11 Treasure of Montezuma
12 Uncle ___
13 Hairpieces
15 Ashram founder's title
16 Hit 1960s sitcom
18 Not *esto* or *eso*
19 Tête de ___ (Swiss cheese whose name means "Monk's Head")
20 Regattas, e.g.
22 Whinny
24 Jazz singer Jones
28 Fellows found in fields
30 Cheyenne's locale: Abbr.
31 Leather from the sea
32 Road trip stop
33 Language suffix
34 Somme *saison*
35 Sarge, for one
36 Rapper Mos ___
37 Abbr. on old maps

DOWN

1 "Ready, ___!"
2 To the left, at sea
3 Gumbel's *Today* successor
4 *Fargo* director Joel
5 Philadelphia product
6 "Fatty" Arbuckle's real first name
7 Buddy of *The Beverly Hillbillies*
8 Poetry
9 *Star Wars: The Phantom Menace* boy
14 City on the Illinois River
17 Choirs may use them
21 "You've got yourself a deal!"
22 *No Strings Attached* pop group
23 Prefix for low-cost items
25 Puffs
26 Nincompoops
27 *JFK* actor
29 Staff symbol
30 Game aim

TOTALLY TUBULAR

ACROSS

4 Crib cry
7 Throw at, as during a football game
10 Once ___ lifetime
11 Tropical flower
12 Ring victories, for short
13 Picks up
15 Martin Landau, in *Ed Wood*
17 Publicist
18 Shady alcove
23 Affections
27 Wandering aimlessly
28 Hurry-scurry
30 Like magma
31 Actress Lupino
32 Perpetual, poetically
33 Lepidopterist's need
34 Rolls back, say

DOWN

1 Sign of indifference
2 Hint of color
3 Takes too much of, briefly
4 User-modifiable website
5 *Mayo* to *mayo*
6 Monopoly maker
7 Gallup undertakings
8 Provinces
9 La ___
14 Laundry crisis
16 Like howls in a haunted house
17 *Nova* network
19 Get back
20 Canadian length
21 "You ___ kidding!"
22 Movie theaters
24 Cooperative witness, maybe
25 Government issue
26 Lollygags
27 Tower of London feature
29 HST's presidential successor

3 ADVICE TO TRAVELERS

```
C A P E M A N . T R A
A T I N G L E . R E M
N E V E R G O . E M I
D I O . . . . A V I S
O N T R I P S W I T H
. . E A R T H . . . .
A N Y O N E Y O U D O
D O E S . . . . C I V
D I N . N O T L O V E
E S T . C R O O N E R
R E L . O S M O N D S
```

4 BACK ORDER

```
S H O J I . S I M P S
P E R O N . H T E S T
A F G H A N I S T A N
. . . A L O H A S . .
O M E N I I . . F A S
M I N N E S O T A N S
S A C . . I N A N E R
. . H A M L E T . . .
S M A R T Y P A N T S
R O N I N . I M O U T
I O T A S . N I T T Y
```

5 CHEERS!

```
E G G E D . S T E I N
B O R E D . P R A D A
O P E R A H O U S E S
O R C . Y A K . E A T
K O O K . M E A S L Y
. . F O S S E . . . .
B R E C H T . R Y A N
L O N . W E T . I M A
D A N G E R A H E A D
G R U E L . S O L T I
S K I L L . M E D I A
```

6 ELEMENTARY

```
I B M . V E G . E T A
O R O . A L E . N E D
W A T E R L O G G E D
A D O R N . . H A T S
. . . A I R T I G H T
S T D . S E E . E E O
E A R T H D A Y . . .
T O Y S . . B E A R D
F I R E S T A R T E R
E S O . T A G . R E A
E M T . Y R S . A F T
```

7 JACKSON 5

```
P Y T . C P A . B E N
L A V . R E M . O R E
A S S . E A T D I R T
N I E C E . R E S O W
S R T A . J A V E R T
. . S N A K E . . . .
A T R I U M . I A G O
D I A N A . A N S O N
L A C O N I C . A T E
I R E . C A R . N A B
B A D . E N E . A B C
```

8 ODD COUPLE

```
H E R O D . E T U D E
B R O M O . L E M O N
O S C A R L E V A N T
. . H E A V Y . . . .
O N R A M P . E L I Z
K I A . I B M . O D E
S A G E . E Y E L I D
. . D E L O N . . . .
F E L I X T H E C A T
A M A T I . M R C U B
O U G H T . Y O L K S
```

9 S CARGO

P	A	N	T	Y		E	C	O	L	I
C	R	O	W	E		V	I	B	E	S
S	P	R	I	N	T	E	R	J	A	M
			S	T	A	N	C	E		
B	A	R	T	A	B		A	C	N	E
O	D	E		S	L	C		T	B	A
A	J	A	R		E	A	T	S	A	T
	S	E	N	A	T	E				
S	H	O	T	M	U	S	T	A	R	D
E	R	N	I	E		I	R	A	T	E
E	S	S	E	X		T	A	S	E	R

10 THREE OF A KIND

A	A	A		C	C	C		E	E	E
S	S	N		I	I	I		P	U	G
L	U	G	G	A	G	E		S	R	O
			R	O	A	R	A	T		
P	O	G	O		R	A	T	E	D	R
P	A	R	T	B		S	H	I	R	R
P	R	O	T	E	M		E	N	T	R
		C	O	S	I	G	N			
H	O	E		T	A	R	S	A	L	S
A	P	R		O	O	O		D	I	E
S	S	S		W	W	W		Z	Z	Z

11 WASH ME

B	A	S	I	L		A	N	E	N	D
A	L	E	R	O		I	N	D	I	E
C	L	E	A	N		S	W	E	E	P
O	E	R		G	A	L		N	C	O
N	Y	S	E		T	E	A	S	E	T
			L	A	S	S	O			
A	S	P	I	R	E		K	A	T	T
U	T	A		G	A	S		G	A	R
D	I	R	T	Y		H	A	R	R	Y
I	N	T	E	L		A	B	E	T	S
S	T	Y	N	E		G	U	E	S	T

12 ATTENTION TO E-TAILS

N	A	T	C	H		C	H	O	R	D
A	P	H	I	D		Y	A	D	D	A
P	R	E	T	T	Y	P	L	E	A	S
		R	E	V	E	R	E			
R	A	I	D		S	U	S	S	E	X
O	A	T		S	O	S		T	W	O
B	A	Z	A	A	R		A	P	E	X
		S	I	N	I	S	E			
M	A	I	N	L	O	B	S	T	E	R
O	R	F	E	O		M	E	E	S	E
S	T	A	R	R		S	T	R	O	P

13 BREW HA-HA

	S	L	A	S	H		U	B	E	R
A	P	O	G	E	E		N	O	M	E
B	E	A	U	T	Y		I	S	I	N
B	E	T	A	S		S	C	E	N	E
O	C	H		T	E	L	E			
T	H	E	E	Y	E	O	F	T	H	E
		S	P	E	W		R	O	W	
A	P	A	C	E		P	E	A	S	E
B	E	E	R		H	O	L	D	E	R
C	A	R	O		S	K	I	E	R	S
S	T	O	W		N	E	E	D	S	

14 DOUBLE TROUBLE

S	A	L	A	A	M		A	C	A	D
I	S	O	L	D	E		S	O	I	R
V	I	S	I	O	N		T	A	K	E
A	N	T	E		D	H	A	R	M	A
		N	O	S	E		S	A	M	
C	R	O	S	S		A	G	E	N	T
H	A	P		L	I	P	O			
A	C	T	I	O	N		W	O	M	B
C	H	I	N		B	O	I	L	E	R
H	E	C	K		O	N	L	I	N	E
I	L	S	A		X	E	D	O	U	T

15 LETTER HEAD

```
S T A G S █ B I D E T
O P R A H █ A P I A N
C S I D E R E S O R T
█ █ █ G E E Z E R S █
S A F E S T █ █ A H A
T W I T H █ L E M O N
Y E R █ █ P I L A T E
█ S E E S O F F █ █ █
I O F T H E T I G E R
E M O T E █ U S E B Y
S E X E D █ P H O B E
```

16 OPPOSITES ATTRACT

```
A B A C I █ G I S M O
A R I A S █ A S L A N
M A R T I N S H O R T
C U E █ T A X █ M I A
O N R A M P █ C O O P
█ █ █ L E T G O █ █ █
H A L T █ I Q T E S T
E T O █ A M T █ R O O
S H E L L E Y L O N G
H O W I E █ P O D I A
E S S E X █ E X E C S
```

17 BATTLE OF THE SEXES

```
T R A S H █ P O A C H
S E R T A █ U N C L E
E L E P H A N T M A N
T I N █ A D J █ E D S
S C A M █ S A W █ █ █
E S S E X █ B E N J I
█ █ █ W R Y █ B O S S
I B M █ A A A █ R B I
P R E T T Y W O M A N
O U T I E █ E X A C T
S T E E D █ D O N H O
```

18 TITLE PAGE

```
S C H M O █ O C C U R
E A T E N █ L O O S E
M R S R O B I N S O N
█ █ █ C R A V A T █ █
H A C K █ Z E N I T H
U R L █ N O R █ N I A
E M I L I O █ M G M T
█ M O N K E Y █ █ █ █
M R B O J A N G L E S
B U E N A █ Z O O E Y
A N D Y S █ O D O R S
```

19 CITY LIGHTS

```
S H O W N █ F A S T S
A U D R A █ R I S K Y
G R E E N B E R E T S
█ █ █ S O L E █ █ █ █
N Y E T █ O U T A G E
Y E L L O W P A G E S
C E L E B S █ G E N T
█ █ █ L I E S █ █ █ █
R E D H O T M A M M A
E N R O N █ I L I A D
B E I N G █ T E N T O
```

20 FORD DEALERSHIP

```
A D A Z E █ H E N R Y
R E T A X █ O R A T E
A C T I I █ R I P E N
F A I R L A N E █ █ █
A G R E E S █ S T R █
T O E █ S T S █ O E R
█ N S C █ E U R O P E
█ █ H A R R I S O N █
L A T I N O █ C O R N
A D O N A I █ C O T E
G E R A L D █ I N S T
```

26 THE I'S HAVE IT

```
H I T █ I N S █ P I N
C R I █ S I X █ M I L
I R R █ I N N █ I L K
I S L I P █ L I N K S
B L I N I S █ T I C S
█ █ █ I S I T I █ █ █
P I T H █ F I N I S H
I N S T S █ K I L T S
H I D █ S M I █ C S I
M R I █ R B I █ C I R
I T D █ S I R █ C G I
```

25 OXYMORONS

```
E L A T E █ S A S S Y
O A S I S █ A N A I S
J U M B O S H R I M P
I S A I D N O █ L E I
G U S H █ I L L E S T
█ █ █ N A S A L █ █ █
L E O I I █ A T M S
E D S █ R A N █ F R E E
B I T T E R S W E E T
A B O M B █ S E L L S
L A N A I █ A D A G E
```

24 IN OR OUT

```
S H A L L █ O N H E R
G U A V A █ O A K I E
P R I V A T E R Y A N
H S T █ P R E T E N D
S H A N I A █ U S S R
█ █ █ I N F E R █ █ █
L E A K █ F R E A K S
A L L O W I N █ M E A
P U B L I C E N E M Y
I D E A L █ S N A P S
S E E I T █ T E N T O
```

23 CROSS WORDS

```
A A H E D █ M A H E R
S T A R E █ A D A M E
H A I R S █ H A T C H
O R R █ O B I █ C E E
W I S E T O █ S H E M
█ █ █ B O N E S █ █ █
C O B B █ E N T R E E
A R R █ E S T █ O D S
B R E E D █ R O A D S
L I E G E █ A N D I E
E N D O N █ P O S E S
```

22 B&B

```
K O I █ B A D █ N O M
I W O J I M A █ E T D
B E T A B L O C K E R
█ A R A B █ T O N I █
N S A █ B I G B A N G
█ █ █ A M E B A █ █ █
D I M █ B E S T B O Y
E M A J █ M E S A
B A T E D B R E A T H
I C E T R A Y █ N E O
T S O █ S H E █ O R S
```

21 PET NAMES

```
P I L A F █ G H O S T
E R I C A █ L O U P E
A T E █ E R R █ C A M
N E R F █ O I L E R S
█ R E P A Y █ █ █ █ █
S Q U I N T █ E A S T
O U R █ Z O O █ N A H
D O G G Y P A D D L E
A T E A M █ T A R O T
S E D G E █ H Y E N A
```

27 CON-JUNCTIONS

S	A	X	O	N		O	R	B	E	D
A	W	A	R	E		K	E	A	N	U
C	A	N	D	W		A	A	N	D	P
K	I	D		T	R	Y		D	U	E
S	T	Y	E		A	E	S	O	P	S
			A	A	N	D	E			
L	I	Q	U	I	D		T	A	T	A
A	N	A		S	R	A		A	I	G
S	A	N	D	L		X	A	N	D	O
E	N	D	U	E		O	G	D	E	N
R	E	A	D	S		N	E	W	S	Y

28 FOUR QUARTERS

S	U	P	P	E	D		A	W	O	L
A	N	Y	H	O	O		M	I	R	O
S	P	R	I	N	G		A	N	E	W
E	C	O	L		M	Y	S	T	I	C
			L	U	A	U		E	D	U
P	L	A	Y	S		C	A	R	A	T
I	O	U		S	A	K	S			
N	A	T	U	R	E		I	A	M	B
O	V	U	M		S	U	M	M	E	R
T	E	M	P		O	R	O	M	E	O
S	S	N	S		P	I	V	O	T	S

29 MUSICAL TRIO

T	I	C		S	I	R		A	F	T
I	D	I		C	L	A	P	P	E	R
P	E	T	E	R	O	T	O	O	L	E
S	A	Y	S	O		E	L	L	S	
		A	L	P	S		L	I	S	
	P	A	U	L	S	I	M	O	N	
C	E	L		S	I	T	E			
O	D	D	S		T	A	S	T	E	
M	A	R	Y	S	H	E	L	L	E	Y
B	L	I	N	K	E	R		A	C	E
S	S	N		I	M	S		V	H	S

30 SAME SURNAME

B	E	T	T	E		M	I	L	E	S
A	L	I	A	S		E	N	E	R	O
B	E	B	O	P		A	C	E	O	F
A	V	E		A	R	T		R	D	A
R	E	T	I	N	A		B	Y	E	S
		D	A	V	I	S				
Y	E	T	I		E	R	A	S	E	S
A	G	O		A	D	V		C	L	I
H	A	R	D	C		I	D	O	L	S
O	D	I	U	M		N	O	N	E	T
O	S	S	I	E		G	E	E	N	A

31 SURROUNDED BY BEES

T	O	R	O	S		D	O	N	A	T
U	V	U	L	A		E	N	O	L	A
B	A	B	E	L		B	E	B	O	P
E	R	E		A	C	T		L	E	E
D	Y	N	A	M	O		B	E	S	S
			B	I	B	L	E			
T	A	L	C		R	U	G	R	A	T
U	N	I		N	A	M		E	L	O
B	O	B	B	Y		B	U	B	B	A
A	U	R	A	S		A	N	E	E	D
S	K	A	T	E		R	O	L	E	S

32 TWO SURE THINGS

P	A	S	T	A		L	A	G	O	S
O	R	C	A	S		E	L	E	N	A
D	E	A	T	H	V	A	L	L	E	Y
S	A	R	A		A	V	I	A	T	E
			S	E	M	E	S	T	E	R
C	S	A		S	O	I		I	N	S
A	P	R	I	C	O	T	S			
S	E	T	T	O	S		T	A	R	A
B	E	F	O	R	E	T	A	X	E	S
A	D	U	L	T		I	S	L	E	S
H	O	L	D	S		T	H	E	F	T

33 CAR TALK

C	O	C	O	A		H	E	A	L	S
O	R	A	L	B		E	L	L	I	E
M	A	K	E	B	E	L	I	E	V	E
E	T	E		A	L	E		R	E	M
T	E	S	T		E	N	C	O	R	E
			L	O	M	A	N			
R	E	S	C	U	E		N	O	R	A
A	C	E		T	N	T		R	A	T
M	O	D	E	L	T	R	A	I	N	S
P	L	A	Y	A		E	R	O	D	E
S	I	N	E	W		K	E	N	Y	A

34 FROM EAR TO EAR

R	O	A	S	T		F	L	O	R	A
A	D	L	A	I		A	A	N	D	E
W	E	A	R	A	N	D	T	E	A	R
			G	R	E	E	K			
B	U	R	E	A	U		E	A	T	S
A	M	A		S	T	L		B	E	N
M	A	S	K		R	A	S	C	A	L
			A	L	O	N	E			
N	E	A	R	A	N	D	D	E	A	R
A	M	P	E	D		A	A	M	C	O
B	O	U	N	D		U	N	I	T	Y

35 ORIENTATION

B	I	L	B	O		B	I	R	T	H
U	T	T	E	R		E	N	E	R	O
S	T	R	A	I	G	H	T	P	I	N
			U	G	L	I	E	R		
B	I	C	S		E	N	L	I	S	T
A	K	A		D	A	D		S	I	R
H	E	R	M	E	S		S	E	X	Y
			R	A	M	O	N	A		
G	A	Y	N	I	N	E	T	I	E	S
O	B	O	E	S		A	A	M	C	O
D	E	N	T	E		T	Y	S	O	N

36 SOUND STAGE

G	A	R	A	G	E		A	J	A	R
A	L	E	R	O	S		L	I	M	E
T	I	P	T	O	P		O	N	I	T
S	T	O	O	D		S	O	G	G	Y
			F	L	I	P	F	L	O	P
C	C	V		U	S	O		E	S	E
C	L	I	P	C	L	O	P			
L	A	S	I	K		N	I	T	R	O
A	M	I	N		H	I	P	H	O	P
M	O	N	K		O	N	E	E	A	R
P	R	E	Y		O	G	R	A	D	Y

37 X-FACTOR

N	A	M		T	D	S		L	E	I
E	C	O		H	A	W		E	N	C
X	R	A	T	E	D	M	O	V	I	E
T	E	N	O	R			V	E	G	A
			M	A	L	C	O	L	M	X
O	P	P		M	A	R		S	A	E
X	R	A	Y	S	P	E	X			
Y	E	Y	E		A	I	M	E	E	
G	E	N	E	R	A	T	I	O	N	X
E	N	O		A	D	O		E	V	A
N	S	W		P	A	R		S	Y	M

38 AFTER "AFTER"

O	R	E		A	S	A		W	O	W
T	A	R		V	C	R		A	D	O
T	H	O	U	G	H	T		S	I	R
E	R	I	N		W	I	S	H	E	D
R	A	C	E		A	S	H			
S	H	A	V	E		T	A	X	E	S
			E	X	T		R	A	L	E
N	A	R	N	I	A		I	N	I	T
O	N	O		T	H	E	F	A	C	T
O	K	S		E	O	N		D	I	E
N	A	E		D	E	S		U	T	E

39 COZY

```
O N D V D ▉ A M I G A
K E E N E ▉ C A N E M
S A F E C R A C K E R
▉ ▉ C R E D E N Z A ▉
S P I K E D ▉ ▉ O E D
S E N S E ▉ P E T R I
S A T ▉ ▉ G R A S S O
S C R E A M A T ▉ ▉ ▉
S O U N D S Y S T E M
S A D T O ▉ T U B E R
S T E R S ▉ O P A L S
```

40 JACKSON 6

```
S H A F T ▉ B A S I C
H O M E O ▉ A G I L E
U N B R E A K A B L E
▉ ▉ ▉ A S S E T ▉ ▉ ▉
D A H L ▉ P R E M I X
R B I ▉ D I Y ▉ D C X
J U M P E R ▉ S T Y X
▉ ▉ ▉ S M I R K ▉ ▉ ▉
U N T H I N K A B L E
N O R A S ▉ O T T E R
I N A W E ▉ S E U S S
```

41 BARE NECESSITIES

```
S C A L D ▉ V A N N A
T H R E E ▉ I D E A L
R O O M S E R V I C E
A P U ▉ I N G A L L S
F I N E ▉ T O N ▉ ▉ ▉
E N D U P ▉ S C A R S
▉ ▉ T O A ▉ E R I N ▉
A P L E N T Y ▉ A P O
B O A R D M E M B E R
E L O P E ▉ T A I N T
L O S E R ▉ I P A S S
```

42 STAPLES

```
M L A ▉ R E P ▉ Q T Y
R A T ▉ E R A S U R E
M Y S T E R Y M E A T
O N E A L ▉ S O U C I
M E A N I E ▉ K E Y S
▉ ▉ ▉ K N A V E ▉ ▉ ▉
S C A T ▉ T A O I S M
T R I O S ▉ C U L P A
R E D P O T A T O E S
A P E S U I T ▉ N E T
W E D ▉ L E E ▉ A D S
```

43 BACK FLIPS

```
O B I ▉ B A A ▉ N C O
R A N ▉ A V E ▉ E L L
A L T ▉ B I R D G O D
L O O P Y ▉ ▉ O R M E
B O W L I N G N I P ▉
▉ ▉ ▉ A N I O N ▉ ▉ ▉
▉ G A N G S T A P A R
R E N E ▉ ▉ O S A G E
T E S T N A B ▉ B I D
E S O ▉ R Y E ▉ S L Y
S E N ▉ A N D ▉ T E E
```

44 IMBEDDED OPPOSITES

```
E T H O S ▉ D O D G E
T R E E T ▉ A C R E S
H A R D O F H E A R T
N U M ▉ P I L A T E S
I M A C ▉ G I N ▉ ▉ ▉
C A N I S ▉ A I D E S
▉ ▉ ▉ R O W ▉ C O M A
A T E C R O W ▉ O B I
W E L L B E H A V E D
A L B E E ▉ A G E R S
Y E A S T ▉ T O R S O
```

45 O CAPTAIN, MY CAPTAIN!

```
A N E W   B A S K E T
T O R I   A T T I L A
H O O K   T E R R O R
O N D I S C   O K I E
M A E   A H A B
E N D E D   N E S T S
      C O O K   P I A
B E N Z   N A I L E R
S N E E R S   K I D D
M O M M I E   E T U I
T W O A C T   A S P S
```

46 SEPARATION

```
A T O M S   I N D E F
S E V E N   N E A T O
P R E N U   P T I A L
E R R   B A A   L I L
N E A P   G R A Y L Y
    B R E A K U P
A V A U N T   G L E E
M I R   S E A   A B S
P O R C U   P I N E S
E L E V E   O P E R A
D A L I S   D O T T Y
```

47 WINNING ROW

```
T S A   E S C   D C L
O T T   F L O   R O O
N O T   F O R   Y O U
S A N Y O   E C O L I
    O R C   O U I S
T I C - T A C - T O E
E N R Y   W O O
T R I O S   A P O L O
H O T   H O T   H O T
E M I   A L E   M I T
R E C   Q E D   S N O
```

48 BOTH SIDES NOW

```
R A G E D   C L A S P
A T A R I   H E N N A
F R O N T L O A D E R
T I L   Z A P   M R S
S A S H   M R H Y D E
    B A B A R
Z A D O R A   S A T E
A P U   M D S   L E D
B A C K P A C K I N G
A C T I I   T E A S E
R E S A T   V A S E S
```

49 EXTREMITIES

```
A F L A C   I O T A S
C R E D O   M O I R A
H A N D P U P P E T S
E M O   S P A   G I S
S E X Y   N I P S E Y
      S T O R E
D E A L E R   A I M E
E N V   E T C   T I L
F O O T T H E B I L L
E L I S E   L A N A I
R A D A R   T H A N E
```

50 MIDDLE LANE

```
T S A R   T I T L E
H O L A   A H C H O O
E N I D   N E U R O N
A A S   A C R   U P S
S T O P T H A T
P A N C H O V I L L A
    B E V E L L E D
R C A   N I N   B A D
H O G T I E   C E D E
O P E R A S   H A I R
S E D A N   I N N S
```

51 RISE AND FALL

```
T I T A N ▓ E T H E R
A M O R E ▓ L E O R A
U P U P A N D A W A Y
R I P ▓ T O E L E S S
U S E R ▓ D R E ▓ ▓ ▓
S H E A F ▓ S A P P Y
▓ ▓ ▓ N A N ▓ F L E A
E M A I L E R ▓ U S C
D O W N T O E A R T H
T N O T E ▓ E X A L T
V A L O R ▓ D E L E S
```

52 VOWEL PLAY

```
P A S T A ▓ U P T O N
E P E E S ▓ N E H R U
S P A C E ▓ S P E E D
K L M ▓ A G E ▓ M O E
Y E S M ▓ R E C E S S
▓ ▓ ▓ S P I N E ▓ ▓ ▓
S T A G E D ▓ O S L O
A I L ▓ A S P ▓ A A A
S P O O N ▓ S P U N K
H I N D U ▓ S I N A I
A N G S T ▓ T E A S E
```

53 LOOK BOTH WAYS

```
O T T O ▓ T A R M A C
O R A L ▓ O R E I D A
M A D A M I M A D A M
P L A Y A ▓ ▓ P A P P
H A S ▓ H O N E S T Y
▓ ▓ ▓ R A D A R ▓ ▓ ▓
L A B E L E D ▓ E N C
A U L D ▓ ▓ I S F O R
I F I H A D A H I F I
R E S O L E ▓ O L E S
D U S T I N ▓ P E E P
```

54 FLYING COLORS

```
H O B O S ▓ M A Y B E
E R A S E ▓ O R E O S
R E D H E R R I N G S
▓ ▓ H A R A S S ▓ ▓ ▓
T S A ▓ ▓ M E T R E S
W H I T E P L A I N S
A U R O R A ▓ ▓ O D E
▓ ▓ ▓ N U G E N T ▓ ▓
B L U E P E N C I L S
K A P U T ▓ V A N Y A
S H I P S ▓ S A G E T
```

55 VACATION PLANS

```
G U S T ▓ D E C A D E
O P T O ▓ I N A R O W
T R E A T M E N I C E
H O R D E ▓ ▓ O A K S
I A N ▓ N A C L ▓ ▓ ▓
C R O P S P R A Y E R
▓ ▓ ▓ R E B A ▓ O L E
W W I I ▓ ▓ I S Y E T
H A N D I N G L O V E
A N G E L A ▓ A M E S
M E A S L Y ▓ W A N T
```

56 ROYAL WE

```
D E E D S ▓ O M E G A
A L I E N ▓ N O M A D
K I N G O F C L U B S
▓ ▓ ▓ A R M E D ▓ ▓ ▓
C H A S E R ▓ Y A R N
O A R ▓ S A C ▓ B E A
Y M C A ▓ D U N C A N
▓ ▓ ▓ H A I R Y ▓ ▓ ▓
Q U E E N O F M E A N
T R E A T ▓ E P S O N
R I N D S ▓ W H O L E
```

57 TWO CANS

```
E R E C T   A A M E S
S E A L Y   B R A V O
S Q U I R T S P R A Y
      P O L O
P L E A   C R A V A T
J E R R Y   B L I T Z
S O R T O F   L I E U
        M I M E
T I N W A T E R I N G
I D I O M   A G R E E
M A N N A   T Y S O N
```

58 BEATLEMANIA

```
R A N C H   I S U Z U
O H Y O U   C O N A N
P A U L R E U B E N S
E S K   R X S   S T U
      E A P   S C A N
J O H N H A N C O C K
I N E S   N U I
G E R   I S M   W O O
G E O R G E B U R N S
L Y I N G   E P E E S
E E N S Y   R I N G O
```

59 DOUBLE STANDARD

```
S E X P O T S   E T S
P R O S A I C   D E T
F O R 2 R T H   E A R
S O O   W O R S E
    A C H I L L E S
O N E H I 2 N D E R S
M O N O T O N E
E V I T A   A P E
L E G   D O N 2 R R Y
E L M   E L E A N O R
T S A   L E T M E B E
```

60 MIXED METAPHOR

```
W E L L   S H A S T A
I D E O   W A S T E D
N U T S   A M A N D A
E A R T H M O P
B R I T A I N   T M I
A D D O N   R O W A N
R O E   G E Y S E R S
      H O P E M A R T
O C T A V O   O K I E
D U P L E X   S E E P
D E S T R Y   E D D S
```

61 SENSE OF DIRECTION

```
C A L C   N A B O R S
O H I O   O N E C U P
A M P S   R E N E G E
L E S T A T   D A R N
    A S H Y   N A T
  W E S T   E A S T
S I M   I S A K
K N I T   O S I R I S
I N L I E U   M I C E
P O I R O T   B T E N
S W O O S H   O A T S
```

62 KIDS!

```
T M I   M O B   A I L
I A M   A K A   H O E
P D A   Z A M B O N I
J E R S E Y B O Y S
A D E N   S I N
R O T I       S A A B
      P R O   A B L E
  D R E A M G I R L S
H O U D I N I   U P S
E N D   S I L   P R E
F E E   E S L   T O S
```

63 RESTAURANT NO-NO'S

D	E	M	O	S		A	M	M	A	N
I	D	A	H	O		S	O	C	I	O
M	U	S	C	L	E	S	H	I	R	T
		R	E	S	T	S				
I	N	T	U	I	T			R	V	S
S	A	D	D	L	E	S	H	O	E	S
H	M	S			L	E	A	N	E	R
		M	O	L	A	R				
R	O	O	M	S	E	R	V	I	C	E
S	T	E	E	L		C	E	N	T	S
T	O	R	S	O		H	Y	D	R	O

64 PAIR OF SOX

F	A	S	C	I	S	M		D	E	F
A	T	L	A	N	T	A		A	L	I
B	O	U	N	C	E	D	C	H	E	X
R	A	M	I	S		D	E	L	V	E
I	S	P	S		M	O	O			
C	T	S		Z	A	G		L	S	T
			W	S	J		B	O	A	R
M	A	F	I	A		H	A	I	T	I
S	W	I	Z	Z	L	E	S	T	Y	X
G	O	D		S	A	L	I	E	R	I
S	L	O		A	S	P	E	R	S	E

65 NOT LYING

R	A	C	E	D		M	A	C	H	O
E	L	U	D	E		O	T	H	E	R
B	A	B	Y	S	I	T	T	I	N	G
U	M	A		O	P	H	E	L	I	A
S	O	N	A	T	A		S	E	E	N
			D	O	N	U	T			
S	C	T	V		E	N	S	I	G	N
T	R	U	I	S	M	S		D	I	I
O	U	T	S	T	A	N	D	I	N	G
I	S	T	O	O		A	D	O	Z	E
C	H	I	R	P		P	E	T	A	L

66 COMEDY DUO

A	T	O	M	S		S	E	C	T	S
M	A	R	I	A		A	M	A	S	S
B	U	R	N	S	R	U	B	B	E	R
		D	E	A	R	E	R			
D	U	T	Y		I	O	D	I	N	E
E	M	U		C	N	N		D	I	D
B	A	R	T	A	B		S	E	X	Y
		T	H	R	O	A	T			
A	L	L	E	N	W	R	E	N	C	H
S	E	E	M	E		M	A	R	T	A
P	O	S	E	Y		S	M	A	R	T

67 RE: PETE

A	D	A	M	S		D	O	D	G	E
D	R	U	M	S		A	R	I	A	L
R	O	S	E	G	A	R	D	E	N	S
O	W	S		T	H	E	E	D	G	E
I	S	I	S		A	M	A			
T	E	E	M	S		E	L	M	E	R
			A	I	L		S	A	M	I
A	L	A	R	M	E	D		N	E	V
B	E	S	T	P	I	C	T	U	R	E
B	A	S	I	L		U	S	A	I	R
A	N	N	E	E		P	A	L	L	S

68 DICHOTOMY

I	O	T	A		K	A	B	O	B	S
D	O	R	M		E	L	E	C	T	S
O	P	E	N	A	N	D	S	H	U	T
		N	I	N	J	A	S			
W	E	T	O	N	E			H	U	M
P	R	O	S	A	N	D	C	O	N	S
M	A	N			N	O	R	T	O	N
		A	C	I	D	I	C			
G	I	V	E	A	N	D	T	A	K	E
I	N	S	O	N	G		I	K	E	S
S	C	O	N	E	S		C	E	R	T

69 PLUSH

```
D I G I T . . T T O P
U N I T E . L A H T I
G A S H S T A T I O N
. . . I T S W A R . .
H O R N E T . . S R O
Q U A K E R O A T H S
S I M . A L L Y O U .
. . P U R P L E . . .
B U S H Y S I G N A L
I N U R E . E R A T O
C O P Y . . S E E M S
```

70 BROKEN PROMISES

```
B A G . F I B . S E Q
A N A . E M O . T R U
S K I . D O O . O N A
E A T M E . T O P A R
. . A X L . P I N T
D A V I . D O R T I Z
A R I Z . R D A . . .
M C G E E . D H A B I
S A O . T V I . D O L
E D D . N I T . A N S
L E A . A M Y . M E A
```

71 KVETCH ME IF YOU CAN

```
Z E L I G . . H A M
E V E R E S T . I K E
B A N A N A S . M A X
. . . G T O S . . .
O L D . N O R I E G A
W O O D Y . A L L E N
S O D A P O P . F L Y
. . G R O G . . . .
D Y E . S L E E P E R
J A R . T E R S E S T
S O S . . A L I C E
```

72 BACK FORMATION

```
H O N E S . P R A M S
A N O D E . H O W I E
G R O U C H O M A R X
G A G . T E N . Y A Y
I M I S S Y O U . . .
S P E E . . T A N G
. . W H A T E V E R
A F B . A M O . E C O
B E A U T Y M A R K S
B L A N C . A P S E S
A L L A H . S U E D E
```

73 B&N

```
J E T T A . T O M E I
I D E A L . O W E N S
B A N J O . B E N C H
E M T . N A E . T I T
. . E S P . D A N A
B I N G O P A R L O R
A N A G . L I E . .
A F R . M E R . S S N
B O N G O . B U N K O
A R I A S . A T E I N
A M A S S . G E E S E
```

74 STAGE BRACKET

```
B A H . E L M . P S T
A G E . N O T . E U R
R U R . L U V . T R U
K E R M I T . C U E S
. . . A S S A U L T S
. B E S T . P L A Y .
T A L K S H O P . . .
O B I S . I S A Y S O
W I T . A R T . R E D
E E E . M E L . L E D
R D S . O D E . Y D S
```

75 DOUBLE STAR

R	O	C	K	Y		R	A	M	B	O
A	R	E	N	A		I	T	A	L	Y
D	R	O	O	L		M	A	S	T	S
			B	I	K	E	R	S		
E	R	A	S	E	R		I	A	N	S
M	O	I		S	E	Z		G	O	O
T	Y	R	A		M	I	S	E	R	Y
	F	I	V	E	P	M				
A	D	A	M	E		L	E	E	L	A
S	I	R	E	N		O	A	T	E	S
S	P	E	E	D		C	R	A	S	H

76 "GEEZ!"

E	G	G	O	S		S	O	G	G	Y
C	L	A	M	P		T	E	A	M	O
Z	I	G	G	Y	M	A	R	L	E	Y
E	D	S		S	E	T		E	N	O
M	E	O	W		T	I	A			
A	S	N	E	R		C	R	A	Z	E
			T	E	D		I	S	A	T
Y	M	A		C	U	T		K	F	C
M	A	G	G	I	E	S	M	I	T	H
C	R	O	A	T		A	R	N	I	E
A	G	G	I	E		R	I	G	G	S

77 SCRAMBLED YEGG

M	A	N	O		S	T	A	T	E	R
A	L	B	A		H	A	V	A	N	A
S	A	C	K	R	A	C	E	R	E	F
			T	O	R	O				
S	C	A	R	C	E		O	M	E	S
A	O	N	E		F	R	E	A	K	
T	O	T	E	M		R	O	S	S	I
			A	M	I		S	T	A	
S	A	F	E	C	R	A	C	K	E	R
A	M	E	C	H	E		H	I	R	E
M	T	H	O	O	D		E	T	N	A

78 DOMESTIC RELATIONS

P	E	G	L	E	G		T	A	L	E
A	R	I	O	S	O		U	L	A	N
T	O	M	S	T	O	P	P	A	R	D
R	I	L	E	D		L	E	N	D	S
I	C	E		Y	U	L				
C	A	T	A	N	D	M	O	U	S	E
			D	O	S		N	I	S	
A	L	T	O	S		S	T	I	N	T
J	E	R	R	Y	G	A	R	C	I	A
A	N	O	N		S	L	I	E	S	T
R	O	D	S		A	T	M	F	E	E

79 THE "IN" CROWD

L	I	G	E	T	N	E		R	V	S
A	R	E	T	H	A	S		O	S	E
H	A	D	D	I	B	S		S	I	C
R	S	S		S	O	I	L	A	G	E
	M	I	B	E	A	R	N	D		
A	L	T	O			N	Y	S	E	
C	A	J	U	S	T	S	E			
C	A	M	E	L	O	T		P	C	T
O	L	A		U	S	O	T	O	U	R
S	A	X		S	E	I	Z	U	R	E
T	A	X		H	A	C	U	T	L	F

80 FILLING STATION

M	D	S		R	E	P		A	P	P
A	A	H		A	M	I		G	E	L
S	H	O	T	G	U	N		A	A	A
S	L	E	W		K	A	S	H	I	
		O	B	S	E	S	S	E	D	
S	A	F	E	T	Y	P	I	N		
A	T	T	E	N	D	E	E			
S	N	E	R	T		C	O	N	K	
K	I	A		S	I	X	T	E	E	N
M	C	S		E	T	E		I	M	O
E	K	E		N	O	S		L	O	X

95

81 MANAGED CARES

S	A	L		C	C	R		E	V	A
E	P	A		O	R	O		B	E	N
T	O	U	P	E	E	S		S	R	I
G	R	E	E	N	A	C	R	E	S	
O	T	R	O		M	O	I	N	E	
		R	A	C	E	S				
	N	E	I	G	H		E	T	T	A
	S	C	A	R	E	C	R	O	W	S
W	Y	O		E	E	L	S	K	I	N
I	N	N		E	S	E		E	T	E
N	C	O		D	E	F		S	S	R

82 TOTALLY TUBULAR

S	T	O		W	A	H		P	A	S
H	I	D		I	N	A		O	R	C
R	N	S		K	O	S		L	E	A
U	G	O	S	I		B	E	L	A	L
G	E	N	T		P	R	E	S	S	A
			A	R	B	O	R			
M	A	C	I	E	S		I	N	T	I
E	R	I	N	G		M	E	A	N	D
T	E	N		A	D	O		M	O	L
R	N	E		I	D	A		E	T	E
E	T	S		N	E	T		R	E	S

ABOUT THE AUTHOR

PATRICK BLINDAUER is a professional puzzle maker (and recovering performer) who resides in Astoria, New York, with the love of his life, Rebecca. His work has appeared in places like *The New York Times*, *The Wall Street Journal*, *The Washington Post*, *Los Angeles Times*, *Games* magazine, and FireballCrosswords.com. As an actor, he has appeared in *Strangers With Candy* and *A Beautiful Mind*.

His other books include *Clue Sudoku*, *Crossword Word Search Puzzles*, *Large Print Sudoku*, *Patricks' Puzzle Pandemonium*, *Scrabble Word Search Puzzles*, *Scratch & Solve Hollywood Hangman*, *Scratch & Solve Word Ladders*, and *Sit & Solve Fun & Easy Crosswords*.

Visit his website, www.patrickblindauer.com, for custom-made crosswords, multi-puzzle contests, and a free monthly crossword.